The Art of Effortless Earning

A Passive Income Journey

by
Jordan P. Masters

The Art of Effortless Earning

A Passive Income Journey

Contents

Embarking on Your Journey to Financial Freedom

Welcome to the first step in transforming your financial life. If you've ever dreamt of breaking free from the daily grind, having more flexibility with your time, and enjoying financial security, you're in the right place. This book is not just about making money; it's about giving you the freedom to live life on your own terms. We're here to equip you with a roadmap to create multiple streams of passive income.

Imagine waking up when you feel like it, pursuing passions that excite you, and not being chained to a nine-to-five job. That's the core essence of financial freedom. It's not just about wealth, but about the liberty to spend your time as you see fit. This book aims to turn that dream into a reality by guiding you step-by-step through various strategies for building passive income streams. We'll cover digital products, real estate, investments, and much more.

But let's manage expectations from the start: achieving financial freedom is neither a get-rich-quick scheme nor an overnight success story. It's a journey filled with learning, adapting, and most importantly, persistence. If you're ready to commit to this journey, you'll find the rewards well worth the effort.

One crucial thing to understand is that passive income is not entirely "passive." Every stream of income you'll build will require an initial investment of time, effort, and sometimes money. The aim is to set up systems that will work for you in the long run, freeing you from

1

the need to always trade your time for money. This shift in mindset—from immediate earnings to long-term wealth—is essential for success.

Why multiple streams of income? The answer is simple: diversification. Relying on just one source of income, even a passive one, can be risky. Multiple income streams can hedge against market downturns, job losses, and other uncertainties. This diversification makes your financial health more resilient and robust.

This book will walk you through various avenues to generate passive income, such as creating digital products, investing in rental properties, and building a dividend portfolio. You'll learn to identify profitable opportunities, execute effective strategies, and optimize your efforts for maximum returns.

Still, the journey to financial freedom isn't solely about tactics and strategies; it's also about cultivating the right mindset. You'll need to embrace patience, persistence, and resilience. Overcoming fear and doubt is part of the process. The mindset shift from an employee to a financially independent individual is significant but entirely achievable with the right tools and mindset.

Before diving into the specifics, it's important to understand your starting point. Assess your current financial situation, set your goals, and educate yourself. Knowledge is your most valuable asset, and continuous learning is imperative. You'll face challenges and setbacks along the way, but with a solid foundation and the right mindset, you can persevere.

One of the key principles we'll focus on is the power of compounding—whether it's in your investments, knowledge, or efforts. Consistent, small actions taken over time can lead to significant results. This principle is at the heart of building sustainable passive income streams.

We'll also cover practical aspects such as setting up the right business structures, understanding taxes and compliance, and protecting your assets. These elements may not be glamorous, but they're essential for ensuring your passive income streams are sustainable and legally sound.

Moreover, we'll address the importance of balancing work and life. Financial freedom isn't just about money; it's also about having the time and mental space to enjoy life. Self-care and continuous learning will be crucial components of your journey. Setting boundaries and maintaining well-being will help you sustain your efforts without burning out.

The journey to financial freedom is personal and unique to each individual. There's no one-size-fits-all approach. This book is designed to offer a range of strategies and insights, allowing you to tailor your path according to your interests, skills, and resources. You'll have the flexibility to pick and choose the methods that resonate most with you.

As we progress, you'll read real-life success stories that demonstrate these principles in action. These stories aren't just inspirational; they provide practical lessons and key takeaways that you can apply in your journey. Learning from others' experiences can fast-track your path to success and help you avoid common pitfalls.

The future is bright for those willing to embrace change and seize opportunities. The landscape of passive income is continually evolving, with new trends and technologies emerging. Staying adaptable and resilient will enable you to capitalize on these trends and keep your income streams thriving.

By the end of this book, you'll have a comprehensive toolkit for financial freedom. You'll be empowered with the knowledge and confidence to build, manage, and optimize multiple streams of passive income, ensuring long-term financial security and independence.

So, if you're ready to take control of your financial future and embark on this transformative journey, let's begin. Financial freedom is within your reach, and this book is your guide to achieving it. Welcome to your new life of limitless possibilities.

Chapter 1:
Understanding Passive Income

The allure of passive income lies in its promise of financial freedom without the constant grind of a 9-to-5 job. Essentially, passive income is the revenue you generate with little to no daily effort—enabling you to earn while you sleep. But achieving this isn't about quick fixes or overnight success; it's about strategically setting up income streams that continue to pay you down the line. Imagine having your money work tirelessly, creating a self-sustaining ecosystem that supports your lifestyle and financial goals. As we journey through this chapter, we'll dismantle common misconceptions, explore real-world examples of successful ventures, and provide a framework for identifying the types of passive income that align with your strengths and interests. Think of passive income as planting seeds that will bear fruit in the future, requiring care and patience but ultimately delivering the freedom to live life on your own terms.

The Myth vs. Reality

When people think of passive income, many imagine a utopian dream where checks roll in while they sip margaritas on the beach. But let's clear that up: it's not as hands-off as it sounds. Yes, the ultimate aim is to minimize ongoing effort, but initial grunt work is essential. Whether it's setting up a rental property, creating a digital product, or building a dividend portfolio, there's often significant time and energy invested up front. The reality is that, while passive income can indeed free you from the 9-to-5 grind, it requires thoughtful planning, hard work, and a consistent effort to manage and optimize. It's not a get-rich-quick scheme but a strategic journey toward long-term financial security and independence. But, once you've laid the foundation, the rewards can be incredibly fulfilling, both financially and personally.

Debunking Common Misconceptions is crucial as you dive into the world of passive income, where myths abound like urban legends around a campfire. These misconceptions can act as roadblocks, deterring you from taking the first step towards financial freedom. So, let's clear the air and set you on the right track.

First up, the notion that passive income requires no effort at all is wildly misleading. Sure, the term "passive" implies less active involvement compared to a 9-to-5 job, but it doesn't mean zero effort. Initial hustle is crucial, whether it's creating an online course, writing an eBook, or setting up a rental property. The effort might taper off, but it never entirely vanishes.

Another myth that often circulates is that you need a lot of money to start generating passive income. This idea can be incredibly discouraging, especially for those with limited resources. The truth is, while some passive income streams, like real estate, may require significant upfront investments, many avenues don't. Options like blogging, affiliate marketing, or creating digital products can be started with minimal financial input.

Many people think passive income is a get-rich-quick scheme, another illusion that needs shattering. Sustainable passive income streams take time to build and mature. You need patience and persistence. It's normal to not see immediate returns, but with consistent effort, the compounding effect can be astonishing.

The belief that passive income is less risky than active income is another misconception. Like any business venture, generating passive income also comes with its own set of risks. Market fluctuations, regulatory changes, and technological disruptions can all impact your income streams. Diversifying your sources of passive income can mitigate some risks but not eliminate them.

Some think passive income is only for the tech-savvy or financially educated. Wrong again. Yes, some understanding of the financial systems can be tremendously helpful, but the barriers to entry are lower than ever. Numerous resources, including this book, provide step-by-step guides to help anyone, regardless of their background, get started.

A pervasive myth is that passive income will suddenly free you from all work-related stress and commitments. While it can provide financial flexibility and reduce the dependency on a fixed paycheck, it doesn't completely eliminate all stress. Managing multiple income streams can be complex, requiring administrative tasks, periodic reviews, and strategic adjustments.

Another common misconception is that you need to have unique, groundbreaking ideas to succeed with passive income. In reality, success often comes from executing existing ideas exceptionally well rather than concocting something entirely new. Identifying a niche, understanding the market needs, and providing high-quality solutions can often yield better results.

The idea that passive income streams are all equal is also misleading. Different types of passive income have varying levels of initial and ongoing effort, risk, and return. For instance, rental income might provide a steady, predictable return but requires significant upfront capital and ongoing management. On the other hand, income from digital products might be less predictable but requires lower initial investment.

Some people think passive income means never having to learn new skills or adapt to new technologies. This could not be farther from the truth. The landscape for generating passive income is continually evolving. Staying updated and adaptable is essential to long-term success. Continuous learning might involve upskilling in digital marketing, understanding new investment tools, or exploring emerging trends like cryptocurrencies.

A particularly dangerous myth is the belief that passive income is only for entrepreneurs. Yes, entrepreneurs might have a head start in understanding the dynamics of making money independently, but passive income is for everyone. Whether you're a teacher, engineer, or stay-at-home parent, anyone can create multiple streams of passive income with the right approach.

Another misconception is that once you've set up a passive income stream, you can completely forget about it. While passive income generally requires less effort than active income, it still needs maintenance. For example, rental properties need upkeep, digital products need updates, and investment portfolios need rebalancing. Regular check-ins ensure that your income streams continue to function efficiently.

Some believe that generating passive income is all about luck. While luck can play a role, the most crucial factor is strategy. Successful passive income earners deploy calculated risks, conduct thorough research, and adapt based on performance metrics. These strategic moves, rather than sheer luck, drive long-term profitability.

The myth that you need to go it alone is another fallacy. Building passive income streams doesn't have to be a solitary journey. Communities, mentorships, and collaborations can amplify your efforts. Sharing expertise, resources, and support can lead to more robust, diversified, and sustainable income streams.

Lastly, it's essential to debunk the myth that passive income guarantees financial freedom overnight. While passive income can give you a way to achieve financial freedom, it does so gradually. It's the steady building, over months and years, that leads to true independence. By debunking these misconceptions, you'll be better equipped to navigate your path to sustainable passive income.

Real-World Examples of Successful Passive Income Streams show us that achieving financial independence is not just a pipe dream. Individuals from various walks of life have accomplished this feat by diligently building and managing multiple streams of passive income. It's one thing to read about strategies and frameworks for generating passive income; it's another to see how these concepts play out in the real world.

Consider the case of Pat Flynn, a name many recognize in the online business community. Flynn's journey into passive income began when he was laid off from his job as an architect. Armed with a blog he had started as a study guide, he transitioned into selling eBooks and online courses about passing architectural exams. His success exemplifies the potential of digital products as a passive income stream. What's more, he leveraged affiliate marketing to diversify his income further, a strategy covered comprehensively in Chapter 7.

Then there's the example of Graeme Hart, a New Zealand businessman. Although not as prominent in mainstream media, his success story is worth noting. Hart utilized dividend investments to generate a steady income stream. Through intelligent stock market investments, he built significant wealth, demonstrating that with the right knowledge and patience, passive income from dividends isn't just for seasoned investors. This strategy's nuances are detailed in Chapter 6.

Jessica and Cliff Larrew are excellent choices to highlight efforts in e-commerce and dropshipping. The couple left their corporate jobs to focus on their online business full-time. They discovered the power of dropshipping, where products are sold without holding inventory themselves. By setting up automated systems to handle order fulfillment, they created scalable income with little ongoing effort. Their achievements emphasize how dropshipping, while requiring initial setup, can become a substantial passive income source as elaborated in Chapter 8.

Another compelling example is Darren Rowse, better known online as ProBlogger. Darren initially started blogging as a hobby, but it wasn't long before he began earning significant revenue through advertising and sponsored content. He strategically focused on niche selection and content strategy, both of which are crucial for blog monetization. Over time, he built a blog empire that now serves as a primary source of passive income, proving that consistent content creation and audience engagement can yield remarkable results. This makes a perfect segue into the discussions in Chapter 9.

Turning our attention to real estate, we find stories like that of Paula Pant. Paula left a traditional 9-to-5 job to pursue real estate investing. She started by purchasing rental properties strategically located in high-demand areas. Efficiently managing these properties and continuously reinvesting her profits allowed her to create a significant passive income stream, freeing her from the constraints of a conventional job. Her success is a testament to the principles discussed in Chapter 4 about getting started with rental properties.

Let's not overlook the realm of YouTube and social media. Take Ryan Higa, a name ubiquitous in the YouTube world. Ryan turned his passion for comedy into a robust YouTube empire. Through ad revenue, merchandise sales, and sponsored content, he built multiple income streams around his online persona. His journey proves that leveraging social media platforms can lead to substantial passive income when approached strategically, a topic explored in depth in Chapter 10.

In the field of stock market investing, we can look up to individuals like Warren Buffett. Although he is primarily known as the Oracle of Omaha for his investing prowess, Buffett's strategy of investing in dividend-paying stocks is a robust passive income model. He reinvests dividends to compound his earnings, demonstrating the power of patience and long-term planning—principles that align with what we discuss in Chapter 6 about building a dividend portfolio.

Patricia Bright, a fashion and beauty influencer, is another example. She diversified her income streams through YouTube revenue, sponsorships, her own product lines, and affiliate marketing. Her success underscores the importance of building a personal brand and using it to create multiple passive income streams, showcasing strategies discussed in Chapter 10 and Chapter 7.

The domain of real estate offers another shining example in Grant Cardone. Grant's mantra of "cash flow is king" led him to acquire multi-family properties that generate significant rental income. His approach to real estate also involves educating others through courses and seminars, adding another layer to his income streams. His experience validates the teachings covered in Chapter 4 about the diverse ways to invest in property.

When examining intellectual property licensing, look no further than Jim Davis, the creator of "Garfield." Licensing the beloved cat for merchandise, films, and TV shows has generated substantial passive income over the years. By capitalizing on intellectual property, Davis turned a creative endeavor into a lasting income source, aligning perfectly with the strategies we'll delve into in Chapter 12.

Private equity and silent partnerships offer less conventional yet lucrative avenues for passive income. Take the example of Peter Thiel, the co-founder of PayPal. Thiel's silent investments in companies like Facebook during its early stages have paid off tremendously. His success illustrates how savvy silent business partnerships, though requiring initial capital, can yield significant passive returns without daily management—a topic covered in Chapter 12.

Airbnb has revolutionized short-term rentals, with hosts like Sarah Lacey embodying its success. Initially, Sarah rented out a spare room, and soon she expanded her offerings to multiple properties. Her strategy involved automating the guest onboarding process, outsourcing cleaning, and leveraging professional photography to market her properties effectively. This approach to Airbnb and short-term rentals delivers a hands-off income stream, a notion elaborated on in Chapter 4.

Let's not forget the world of software and mobile applications. Joel Comm provides an inspiring story here. Joel developed the iFart app, which may sound trivial but has brought in significant revenue with minimal ongoing effort. His story reaffirms that sometimes simple ideas, when executed well, can lead to substantial passive income, capturing the essence of entrepreneurship that we'll explore in Chapter 5.

Lastly, consider the founders of major subscription-based services like Reed Hastings of Netflix. Hastings saw a gap in the market for convenient, subscription-based access to quality content. Creating a service with enormous scalability, he has generated an ongoing revenue stream that grows with each new subscriber. His success highlights the potential of subscription models, something akin to the recurring revenue that can be built through a well-implemented email marketing strategy, elaborated in Chapter 11.

The varied yet successful experiences of these individuals illustrate that the path to financial freedom through passive income is diverse and achievable. By studying their journeys and adopting a blend of strategies, you too can create sustainable, long-term income streams. The wealth of examples shows us that the road to financial freedom isn't reserved for the few but is accessible to anyone committed to taking action.

Types of Passive Income

Understanding the different types of passive income is crucial if you're looking to escape the 9-to-5 grind and achieve financial freedom. Essentially, passive income can be derived from a variety of sources, each with its unique benefits and entry requirements. Whether it's earning money through *digital products* like eBooks and online courses, generating *rental income* from real estate properties, or earning *investment dividends* from stocks and mutual funds, the idea is to create streams of revenue that require minimal continuous effort. By diversifying across these multiple income streams, you not only increase your earnings potential but also mitigate risks. Knowing what options are available allows you to strategically choose methods that align with your skills, interests, and financial goals. This knowledge empowers you to build a sustainable network of passive income streams, setting the stage for long-term financial security and independence.

Digital Products represent one of the most innovative and accessible avenues for generating passive income in today's digital age. Why? Because they can be created once and sold indefinitely without the need for physical inventory, shipping, or even much ongoing maintenance. This makes them an appealing choice for anyone seeking to break free from the traditional 9-to-5 grind.

First off, what exactly are digital products? Digital products are intangible assets or pieces of media that can be sold and distributed repeatedly online. Think eBooks, online courses, software, mobile apps, printables, or even licensing of digital art and music. You're essentially leveraging knowledge, skills, and creativity to build products that have a wide-reaching impact—and the best part is, your market is the entire internet.

Creating digital products requires an investment of time and effort up front, but the long-term benefits can be substantial. They offer the allure of scalability without the constraints of traditional product-based businesses. An eBook, for example, can be sold to ten people or ten thousand people with no additional effort from you. The same goes for an online course; once it's up and running, your primary task is just to manage marketing and customer support.

A critical first step in creating a digital product is identifying your niche. Your niche should be an intersection of what you're passionate about and what people are willing to pay for. If you have specialized knowledge in a certain area—say, digital marketing, coding, or fitness—you can translate this into a product that provides value to others. The key is to pinpoint a specific problem or need and then create a solution in digital form.

Now, let's talk about eBooks. EBooks are a fantastic entry point for many aspiring passive income earners. You don't need to be a published author or have a formal background in writing; what you need is valuable content that people are willing to pay for. Once written, your eBook can be distributed through various platforms such as Amazon Kindle, your own website, or other third-party sellers. The scalability of eBooks makes them an ideal passive income source.

Next up are online courses. With the rise of e-learning platforms like Udemy, Teachable, and Coursera, creating and selling an online course has never been easier. If you possess unique skills or knowledge, packaging that into a structured course can provide significant passive income. From producing video lessons to creating PDFs and quizzes, there are multiple formats you can use to enrich the learning experience.

Software and mobile applications also fall under the umbrella of digital products, albeit requiring a slightly different skill set. This category isn't constrained to coders alone; even if you have an idea but lack the technical skills, you can collaborate with a developer. Once developed, your software or app can generate revenue through sales, subscriptions, or in-app purchases.

Marketing is another key aspect to focus on. You could have the most valuable product, but without effective marketing, it won't reach your target audience. This involves understanding your audience, creating compelling content, and utilizing various marketing channels like social media, email marketing, and SEO. A well-executed marketing plan can significantly amplify your digital product sales.

One significant advantage of digital products is the low overhead costs. Unlike physical products, you don't need a warehouse, inventory, or a large team to manage operations. Most of the costs are upfront—like content creation or development—but once the product is live, the maintenance costs are minimal. This allows for greater profit margins over time.

Digital products also benefit from the "evergreen" factor. Once your product is out there, it can continue to sell for years with minor updates and improvements. For instance, an online course on a subject like photography basics won't become outdated quickly, and you can make small updates periodically to keep it fresh.

When you start seeing steady income from your digital products, you'll taste the sweet freedom that comes from having money work for you. This freedom lets you explore other interests, spend time with loved ones, or even venture into creating additional digital products to diversify your income streams further. The cycle of creation, marketing, and earning perpetuates itself, giving you a reliable stream of passive income.

The beauty of digital products lies in their ability to evolve. As you gather feedback from users, you can make improvements, introduce new features, or even create supplementary products. This adaptability ensures that your offerings remain relevant and valuable over time.

However, it's important to acknowledge potential challenges. Reaching your target audience can be tricky amidst the noise of the internet, and continuous marketing efforts are essential. Additionally, staying updated with ever-changing technologies and market trends requires ongoing learning and adaptation. But, with determination and a strategic approach, these challenges are manageable.

Ultimately, digital products embody the essence of passive income—they represent a powerful way to leverage your expertise and creativity to generate ongoing revenue. By investing your skills and knowledge into creating valuable digital assets, you're not only building financial security but also contributing to a culture of shared knowledge and innovation. So, roll up your sleeves, start brainstorming, and take the first step toward transforming your ideas into profitable digital products.

Rental Income, one of the most time-tested and proven methods for generating passive income, is often the cornerstone of a robust financial independence strategy. At its core, rental income involves acquiring real estate properties and leasing them to tenants who pay you rent, providing a steady income stream. This form of passive income not only contributes to your financial freedom but also has the potential to appreciate in value, creating a dual benefit over time.

The allure of rental income lies in its predictable and largely passive nature. Once you've navigated the initial hurdles of property purchase, renovation, and tenant acquisition, the income generated is relatively hands-off. Of course, this isn't to say it's entirely effortless—managing tenants, maintaining properties, and ensuring timely rent collection all require attention. However, these responsibilities can be outsourced to property management companies, further cementing the passive aspect of this income stream.

One major advantage of rental income is the tangible asset backing it. Unlike other forms of passive income, such as digital products or investments that can fluctuate heavily, real estate is a physical asset that you can leverage, sell, or refinance if needed. This adds a layer of security and robustness, making it an indispensable part of any diversified passive income portfolio.

When diving into rental properties, the phrase "location, location, location" couldn't be more accurate. The geographic area of your property significantly influences demand, rental rates, and long-term value. Urban areas, places near educational institutions, and neighborhoods with low crime rates tend to attract reliable tenants willing to pay higher rents. Research is key—studying market trends, comparable rental rates, and future development plans for the area can give you a considerable edge.

Financing your first rental property can be a daunting task, but it's also a critical step. Various financing options like conventional mortgages, FHA loans, or even hard money loans are available, though each comes with its own sets of terms, interest rates, and duration. Striking a balance between loan terms and your financial capacity is crucial for long-term viability. Leverage your financial literacy to negotiate better terms and understand the impact of interest rates on your investment.

Once the property is secured and ready for occupancy, tenant management becomes the next frontier. Proper tenant screening can save countless future headaches. Running background checks, verifying employment, and checking prior rental history are just some of the steps to ensure you have reliable tenants. Should you decide to not manage the property yourself, hiring a trustworthy property management company can handle everything from tenant screening to maintenance, considerably minimizing your day-to-day involvement.

Marketing your rental property effectively is just as important as the property itself. Using platforms like Zillow, Craigslist, and social media can help you reach a wider audience. Professional photos, compelling descriptions, and competitive pricing will attract high-quality tenants more quickly. Don't underestimate the power of word-of-mouth and referrals within the community as they often yield some of the most reliable tenants.

Another approach to enhancing your rental income is considering short-term rentals through platforms like Airbnb. This model can often generate higher returns compared to traditional long-term leases. However, it requires more management—in terms of guest turnover, cleaning, and ensuring the property meets local regulations. That said, the extra income can often justify the additional work or the cost of hiring a management service specifically for short-term rentals.

Once your rental property is up and running, keeping a keen eye on cash flow is essential. Monitor your income and expenses diligently to ensure profitability. Regular maintenance, property taxes, insurance, and potential vacancies all need to be accounted for. Maintaining a contingency fund for unexpected repairs or vacancies can mitigate financial strain and ensure the rental property remains a positive income source.

Scaling your rental property portfolio can exponentially increase your passive income, but it's not without its risks. Diversifying across different types of properties—residential, commercial, multi-family units—can help spread risk and maximize returns. Using the equity in your current properties to finance new acquisitions is a common strategy, albeit one that requires sound financial judgment.

Appreciation is another significant benefit that rental properties offer. Over time, the value of your property is likely to increase, providing both increased rental income and potential capital gains if you decide to sell. In addition, property upgrades and improvements can further enhance its value, offering a means to increase the monthly rent or resale value.

Understanding the tax implications of rental income is another vital component. Tax benefits such as mortgage interest deductions, property depreciation, and operational cost deductions can signifycantly improve the profitability of your rental properties. Consulting a tax advisor who specializes in real estate can provide insights tailored to your specific situation and help maximize your after-tax returns.

Legal considerations can't be ignored. Renting properties involves contracts, tenants' rights, and local laws that must be respected. Standardized lease agreements, awareness of eviction laws, and staying updated on local rental regulations are crucial for smooth operations. Legal disputes can be costly and time-consuming, so preventive measures and legal advice are advisable.

Tenant retention is an often overlooked aspect of rental income. High tenant turnover can eat into profits through additional marketing costs, vacancy periods, and maintenance. Fostering good relations with tenants, addressing their concerns promptly, and providing a well-maintained living environment can lead to long-term, satisfied tenants and stable income.

Rental Income is a powerful tool on your journey to financial freedom. It not only provides a reliable income stream but also offers potential appreciation and tax benefits. With careful planning, effective management, and strategic scaling, rental properties can become a cornerstone of your passive income portfolio, helping you achieve financial independence and long-term security.

Investment Dividends are often hailed as the holy grail of passive income, and for good reason. When approached strategically, investing in dividends can transform your financial landscape, providing a steady stream of income with minimal ongoing effort. But before you dive headfirst into the world of dividend investing, it's crucial to understand the mechanics, benefits, and potential pitfalls.

At its core, dividend investing involves purchasing shares of established companies that distribute a portion of their earnings back to shareholders in the form of dividends. These payouts can be in the form of cash or additional shares, and they're typically distributed on a quarterly basis. Imagine earning money just for holding onto stocks you own—sounds like a dream, right?

One of the most compelling aspects of dividend income is its potential for reliability. Unlike flipping real estate or managing an e-commerce store, dividend investing doesn't require active involvement once you've made your initial investments. You essentially become part-owner of profitable corporations, enjoying the fruits of their success without lifting a finger.

However, not all dividends are created equal. When selecting dividend-paying stocks, you should look for companies with a track record of consistent, stable payouts. Companies in sectors such as utilities, consumer goods, and healthcare often fit this profile, providing steady returns even during economic downturns. This stability is what can make dividend stocks a cornerstone of a balanced investment portfolio.

But don't let the allure of regular payouts cloud your judgment. It's important to conduct thorough research before committing your hard-earned money. Key factors to examine include the company's dividend yield, payout ratio, and historical performance. A high yield might seem attractive, but it could also signal financial instability or unsustainable payout practices. Balance is key.

When starting your dividend portfolio, diversification is crucial. By spreading your investments across various sectors and industries, you mitigate the risk associated with downturns in any single market. This way, even if one industry faces challenges, your overall income stream remains robust and secure.

To further enhance your dividend strategy, consider reinvesting your dividends through a Dividend Reinvestment Plan (DRIP). These plans allow you to automatically use dividend payouts to purchase more shares of the company, effectively compounding your returns over time. It's a powerful way to grow your portfolio without additional cash input.

Tax considerations are another essential aspect of dividend investing. Dividend income is generally taxable, but the rate can vary depending on whether the dividends are qualified or non-qualified. Understanding the tax implications can help you maximize your after-tax income and avoid unpleasant surprises come tax season.

New investors often wonder how much capital is needed to get started with dividend investing. The truth is, you can begin with relatively modest sums. Thanks to fractional shares and commission-free trading platforms, building a dividend portfolio has never been more accessible. The key is to start small, remain consistent, and let time work its magic.

Despite its many advantages, dividend investing isn't entirely risk-free. Market volatility can impact stock prices and, consequently, dividend payouts. Economic downturns or company-specific issues may lead to dividend cuts or suspensions. Thus, staying informed about the companies you invest in is vital for maintaining a healthy portfolio.

Moreover, don't overlook the importance of liquidity. While dividend stocks can be sold relatively quickly, market conditions can affect timing and pricing. Having a comprehensive exit strategy ensures you won't be caught off guard if you need to liquidate your holdings.

One often-overlooked benefit of dividend investing is the potential for dividend growth. Many companies not only offer dividends but increase them annually. Investing in such companies can lead to a growing income stream, providing a hedge against inflation and increasing your purchasing power over time.

It's also worth noting the psychological advantages. Knowing you're receiving regular income without ongoing effort can provide peace of mind and financial security. This can be particularly rewarding for those looking to supplement retirement savings or achieve early financial independence.

In summary, dividend investing offers a blend of reliability, growth potential, and low-maintenance management. By carefully selecting and diversifying your investments, reinvesting earnings, and staying informed, you can create a sustainable income stream that supports your journey toward financial freedom. Always remember, every dollar invested is a step closer to breaking free from the 9-to-5 grind, making every effort you put into understanding and optimizing this income stream worthwhile.

Chapter 2:
The Mindset Shift

As we transition from understanding what passive income is in theory to actually building diversified income streams, it's crucial to undergo a fundamental mindset shift. Picture your current financial life as a plant that's been watered with active income, trading time for money. The goal now is to transform that plant into a self-sustaining ecosystem that grows even when you're not watering it directly. This shift involves moving from a mindset of immediate gratification to one where patience and persistence are key. You'll trade short-term gains for long-term wealth, cultivating a sense of resilience as you face inevitable setbacks. Overcoming fear and doubt is not just an option, it's a necessity for anyone looking to break free from the 9-to-5 grind. Embrace the unknown with a hopeful heart, allowing yourself to dream bigger and work smarter. After all, financial freedom isn't just a destination—it's a journey shaped by the mindset you adopt today.

From Active Earnings to Passive Wealth

Transitioning from active earnings to passive wealth is a radical shift in mentality and strategy. This transformation isn't solely about changing how you make money; it's about changing how you think about money.

Many of us are conditioned to equate earning money with trading time for dollars. The more hours we work, the more money we make, right? That's the traditional narrative. But there's a cap to this approach: we only have so many hours in a day. Eventually, you hit a ceiling and burn out becomes an inevitable risk.

What if, instead, you made money while you slept, traveled, or spent time with loved ones? This isn't a fairy tale—it's a viable reality with the right mindset and approach. Passive income allows you to earn money without having to be directly involved in the day-to-day operations. Imagine multiple revenue streams consistently flowing in, diminishing your dependency on any single source of income.

This is where the mindset shift comes in. Moving from active earnings to passive wealth requires a significant change in how you perceive financial opportunities. For starters, you need to cultivate a mentality geared towards seeing money as a tool that can work for you, not just as something you work for.

Transitioning into passive income streams starts with recognizing the power of leverage. Leverage is using resources—whether they be time, money, or knowledge—in a way that multiplies their effect. Real estate, for instance, can be a robust lever. A single rental property can provide a steady cash flow that requires minimal active involvement once set up. Similarly, digital products like eBooks or online courses can sell on autopilot.

A crucial component of this mentality is delayed gratification. Passive income building often requires upfront effort and investment. There's a substantial initial time or financial commitment, but the long-term rewards far outweigh the upfront sacrifices. Think about writing a book: it takes time and persistence, but once published, it can generate income for years.

Now, patience is another virtue you'll need to embody fully. Unlike active income, which provides immediate financial gratification, passive income can take months or even years to manifest fully. It's essential to stay the course and keep your eye on the bigger picture. The slow and steady growth may not seem exciting at first, but it's the underpinning of lasting financial security.

Risk tolerance also plays a vital role. Investing in passive income streams implies taking calculated risks. However, these risks can be mitigated with adequate research, proper financial education, and a diversified income strategy. The idea is not to put all your eggs in one basket but to distribute your risk along various income avenues.

An essential step in this transition is continuous self-education. The world of passive income is dynamic, filled with opportunities like real estate, stock investments, digital products, and more. The more you learn, the better decisions you'll make, and over time, the less risky your ventures will become. Remember, knowledge isn't just power—it's profit.

Another critical mindset shift is viewing failures as learning experiences rather than setbacks. Not every venture will pan out the way you hope, and that's okay. Each stumble provides invaluable lessons that you can apply to future endeavors. Thomas Edison famously said, "I have not failed. I've just found 10,000 ways that won't work." Adopting a similar mindset will prepare you to navigate the ups and downs in your journey toward passive wealth.

Next, let's talk about the importance of optimizing and automating. For passive income to truly become "passive," automating processes is crucial. Whether it's through technology, outsourcing, or strategic partnerships, the goal is to minimize active management. For instance, automated email marketing campaigns for a digital product can run 24/7, converting leads into customers seamlessly.

Mindset shifts also include recognizing the value of outsourced skills. The DIY approach can only get you so far. To scale your income streams, you might need to hire experts in various fields—whether for content creation, marketing, or even managing investment properties.

These experts can free up your time to focus on strategic, big-picture tasks that will propel your passive income forward.

Moreover, cultivating a community or network of like-minded individuals can provide invaluable insights and encouragement. Engaging with a community that understands the principles of passive wealth can offer support, share strategies, and even present collaboration opportunities. It's about leveraging collective wisdom to pave your path more effectively.

Lastly, the journey from active earnings to passive wealth is a lifestyle change, not just a financial one. You'll need to adjust your priorities, focusing more on long-term gains rather than immediate returns. This shift will not only provide financial freedom but also the liberty to live life on your terms.

In sum, moving from active earnings to passive wealth is a multifaceted approach that requires a thorough change in mindset. It involves embracing leverage, patience, risk tolerance, continuous self-education, learning from failures, optimizing and automating processes, valuing outsourced skills, cultivating a supportive community, and adjusting your lifestyle for the long haul. By internalizing these principles, you're well on your way to achieving sustainable financial independence.

Cultivating Patience and Persistence

In your journey towards achieving financial freedom through passive income, one of the most crucial shifts you'll need to make is cultivating patience and persistence. The road isn't always smooth, and there's no magic formula that will yield instant results. Passive income streams take time to build and often require a great deal of trial and error. Yet, the rewards are well worth the effort. Let's dig into why patience and persistence are critical and how you can develop these traits.

First, it's important to acknowledge that building passive income is a long-term game. Just as a farmer plants seeds and waits for months before harvesting crops, you'll also need to sow the seeds of your passive income streams and wait for them to grow. This means continuous effort and consistent input, even when you don't see immediate returns. Keeping your eye on the larger picture can help you stay motivated. Think of it as delayed gratification; the more you cultivate patience, the sweeter the fruits of your labor will be.

Patience often means resisting the temptation to quit when results don't come as quickly as you'd hoped. It's easier said than done, especially when you're putting in hard work and seeing little to no returns. This is a part of the entrepreneurial journey that separates those who succeed from those who don't. The hurdles and setbacks you face are not signs to give up but stepping stones to learn from. Real growth happens in these challenging moments, and your ability to stay the course will define your success.

A practical approach to cultivating patience is setting realistic expectations. It's not uncommon for people to think that passive income systems will generate substantial income almost immediately. While it's possible to start seeing some returns in a few months, substantial results usually take years. Understanding this timeline from the beginning can help manage your expectations and keep frustration at bay.

Persistence, on the other hand, is all about maintaining steady effort towards your goals, even in the face of obstacles. It's not enough to be patient; you also have to be relentless. This means learning from setbacks and continuing to adapt and innovate. Successful passive income earners often emphasize the importance of persistence. They didn't achieve financial independence overnight. Instead, they reached their goals by consistently moving forward, even when the going got tough.

One of the best ways to stay persistent is by creating a plan and sticking to it. Detailed plans break down large, overwhelming goals into smaller, manageable tasks. This makes it easier to stay on track and measure your progress. Reviewing your plan regularly can also help you identify what's working and what needs adjustment. This flexibility ensures that you're always moving in the right direction, even if it means taking a few detours along the way.

Create routines that support your goals. Routines instill discipline, which is essential for persistence. For instance, you might set aside a specific time each week to work on your passive income projects. By doing so, you make progress a part of your life, rather than a sporadic activity. This habit-building not only keeps you on track but also gradually turns effort into results.

It's also vital to celebrate small victories. Each milestone reached, no matter how minor, is a step closer to achieving your ultimate goal. Recognizing and appreciating these small successes can boost your motivation and reinforce your commitment. This kind of positive reinforcement makes the journey much more enjoyable and sustainable.

Another aspect of persistence is continuous learning. The landscape of passive income is always evolving, with new opportunities and challenges emerging regularly. Staying updated with industry trends, learning new skills, and applying new knowledge to your endeavors can keep you ahead of the curve. This means reading relevant books, engaging in forums, taking courses, and even finding a mentor who has walked the path you're on.

Mental resilience is another cornerstone of persistence. You'll inevitably encounter naysayers, doubters, and even your internal critic telling you it's not possible. Developing mental toughness helps you stay focused on your goals despite these distractions. This resilience often comes from a strong "why" — knowing why you're pursuing financial freedom through passive income and keeping that motivation front and center.

Your network can also be a significant source of strength. Surround yourself with like-minded individuals who understand your goals and share similar aspirations. Being part of a supportive community can provide encouragement, advice, and even collaboration opportunities. Networking with others on the same path can make the journey less lonely and more engaging.

Let's not forget the importance of adaptability in persistence. The path to building passive income is rarely linear. Market conditions change, new competitors emerge, and initial strategies may not pan out as expected. Being adaptable means you can pivot and tweak your approach without losing sight of your ultimate goals. It's about being persistent in your mission but flexible in your methods.

Moreover, cultivate a positive mindset. Keeping an optimistic outlook even when things are tough can make a world of difference. Focus on solutions rather than problems, and view challenges as opportunities to grow. A positive mental attitude can provide the energy and enthusiasm needed to push through difficult periods.

Lastly, never underestimate the power of taking care of yourself. Achieving financial freedom isn't just about the end result; it's also about enjoying the journey. Make sure you balance your efforts with proper rest, exercise, and leisure activities. A well-rounded, healthy lifestyle can provide the stamina and mental clarity needed to stay persistent and patient over the long run.

In summary, cultivating patience and persistence is indispensable in your journey to financial freedom through passive income. These traits will help you navigate setbacks, manage expectations, and ultimately stay on course. Remember, the seeds you're planting now will lead to a harvest of financial independence in the future. So, keep nurturing them with patience, watering them with persistence, and you'll eventually see the fruits of your labor.

Overcoming Fear and Doubt

The path to financial freedom is paved with both opportunities and challenges. When you're looking to transition from a traditional 9-to-5 job to establishing multiple streams of passive income, fear and doubt can become unwelcome companions. It's essential to recognize and address these feelings because they have the potential to derail your efforts before you even begin. But let's explore how you can effectively overcome these obstacles and cultivate a mindset that propels you toward your goals.

First, understand that fear and doubt are natural human responses to change and uncertainty. We're wired to seek safety and predictability, and venturing into unfamiliar financial terrain can trigger a range of emotions. Acknowledge these feelings without judgment. They don't define you; they merely point to areas where you need more information or a shift in perspective.

The most effective way to combat fear and doubt is through knowledge. When you educate yourself about passive income strategies, the market, and potential risks, you diminish the unknown. Knowledge turns a nebulous, intimidating concept into something tangible and actionable. Make it a habit to learn continuously—whether through books, courses, or networking with experienced individuals.

Remember, everyone starts somewhere. The success stories you read about didn't happen overnight. They were built on patience, persistence, and the willingness to embrace uncertainty. Rather than seeing doubt as a barrier, view it as a marker that you're stepping outside your comfort zone, which is a critical step for growth.

Another powerful tool to overcome fear is visualization. Picture your life after achieving financial independence. Imagine the freedom you will have, the choices you can make, and the security you'll feel. Visualization can serve as a motivational force, helping you stay focused during challenging times. The more vividly you can imagine your success, the more real and achievable it becomes.

Breaking down your goals into smaller, manageable steps can also alleviate anxiety. A grand vision can sometimes feel overwhelming, but when you divide it into actionable tasks, it becomes less daunting. Each small win builds momentum and confidence. Celebrate these small victories as they represent progress towards your ultimate goal of financial freedom.

It's also crucial to build a support system. Surround yourself with like-minded individuals who understand your journey and can offer encouragement and advice. Join forums, attend workshops, or engage with online communities focused on passive income and financial independence. A supportive network can provide fresh perspectives, share valuable insights, and bolster your morale when doubts arise.

Don't underestimate the power of a positive mindset. Cultivate an attitude of optimism and resilience. Understand that setbacks are part of the process. They provide learning opportunities and pave the way for better strategies. When you approach challenges with a solutions-oriented mindset, you mitigate the power of fear and doubt.

Moreover, consider the cost of inaction. Remaining in a state of hesitation and doubt can be more detrimental than taking calculated risks. The comfort of a steady job may offer short-term security but can prevent you from realizing your long-term potential. Reflect on what you're sacrificing by letting fear dictate your choices.

Mindfulness practices, such as meditation and journaling, can help manage stress and maintain focus. These practices enable you to stay grounded and invest your energy in constructive actions. They provide clarity, helping you discern between irrational fears and legitimate concerns that require attention.

It's also beneficial to seek mentorship. Learn from those who have successfully navigated the journey you're embarking on. Mentors can offer priceless advice, share their own experiences with fear and doubt, and provide a reality check to dispel unrealistic fears.

Financial literacy is another critical component in overcoming doubt. Understanding how money works, how investments grow, and the principles of risk management can provide peace of mind and empower you to make informed decisions. Equip yourself with financial tools and knowledge to build a solid foundation for your passive income streams.

Finally, embrace an experimental mindset. Understand that not every endeavor will succeed, and that's okay. Treat each effort as an experiment with valuable lessons. This approach diminishes the fear of failure by framing it as a step towards eventual success. The key is to stay adaptable and continuously refine your strategies based on what you learn.

Overcoming fear and doubt is a process, not a one-time effort. As you progress, these feelings may resurface, but with the right strategies and mindset, they won't hold you back. Stay committed to your vision, keep learning, and surround yourself with supportive and knowledgeable people. Your journey to financial freedom is a testament to your courage and determination, and by confronting fear and doubt head-on, you lay the groundwork for long-term success.

Chapter 3:
Laying the Foundation

Building a reliable passive income stream starts with a solid foundation, and that begins with clear, actionable goals. Without specific targets, your journey to financial independence may feel aimless. Next, it's crucial to understand your current financial situation — your assets, liabilities, income, and expenses. Knowing where you stand will help you formulate a practical strategy tailored to your unique circumstances. Equipping yourself with financial literacy is equally essential. Understanding basic financial concepts allows you to make informed decisions, mitigate risks, and seize opportunities. Think of this chapter as crafting the bedrock upon which you'll construct a robust, passive income portfolio. Together, these elements form the pillars that will support every income stream you build and allow you to navigate the path to financial freedom with confidence and direction.

Goal Setting for Long-Term Success

Mastering passive income requires clear, focused goals. These goals aren't just arbitrary milestones; they're the very foundation that supports and guides your journey towards financial independence. Without them, it's easy to get derailed or distracted. The process of setting these goals is where we begin laying the concrete path to your financial future.

First off, let's emphasize the importance of **specificity** in goal setting. Vague goals like "I want to be rich" won't cut it. To make your goals actionable, they need to be specific. Instead of aiming to "earn more money," target "earning $5,000 a month in passive income within three years." The more precise your goal, the clearer the steps to achieve it.

Equally critical is the element of *measurability*. How will you know when you've achieved your goal? Setting measurable goals means quantifying them in ways that allow you to track your progress. This could be the amount of income, the number of properties acquired, or even the metrics associated with your digital products.

Ambition is a good thing, but your goals should also be **achievable**. Aim for the stars, but ground your aspirations in reality. Unrealistic goals will only lead to disappointment and may deter you from continuing on your path. It's essential to consider your current skills, time, and resources when defining what's achievable.

Relevance is another cornerstone. Your goals should align with your broader life objectives. Consider why you want financial freedom—whether it's to spend more time with family, travel the world, or simply enjoy peace of mind. When goals are relevant, they resonate more, fueling your motivation to reach them.

Finally, your goals need to be *time-bound*. Deadlines create a sense of urgency and help you stay focused. Setting a timeframe—such as a year, three years, or five years—keeps you in check and helps break down your overarching goals into manageable chunks. Short-term goals serve as the building blocks, keeping you motivated en route to your long-term ambitions.

Once your goals are set, the next step is to create a strategic plan. This is where you map out the step-by-step actions required to reach those goals. Think of it as your financial roadmap. For instance, if one of your goals is to generate passive income through rental properties, your plan might include researching markets, saving for down payments, and finding reliable property managers.

Equally important is to **regularly review** and adjust your goals and strategies. Life is dynamic, and so are your circumstances. As you progress, some goals might need tweaking. Set frequent check-ins—quarterly or bi-annually—to measure your progress and refine your plans. It's a continuous process of assessment and adjustment.

Understanding your personal strengths and weaknesses can significantly influence your goal-setting process. Conducting a self-assessment helps identify where you can excel and where you may need help. Evaluating your current situation with brutal honesty aids in setting realistic and achievable goals.

As you embark on this journey, surrounding yourself with a network of supportive individuals can make a monumental difference. Whether it's mentors, peers, or online communities, sharing your goals and progress with others can provide added motivation and accountability. Remember, it's easier to stay committed when you have people who believe in your vision.

Don't overlook the psychological aspect of goal setting. Visualizing success can be a powerful motivator. Create a vision board or write a detailed description of your future life once you achieve your financial goals. These visual cues can serve as daily reminders of why you're putting in the effort now.

Of course, it's crucial to celebrate milestones along the way. Recognizing and rewarding yourself for achieving smaller goals can provide the encouragement needed to keep pushing forward. These celebrations don't have to be extravagant; even small rewards can reinvigorate your drive.

Remember to stay flexible and adaptable. The financial landscape is ever-changing, and rigidly adhering to a plan without room for adaptability might set you back. By being agile, you can seize unforeseen opportunities and navigate around obstacles more effectively.

Your personal growth goes hand-in-hand with financial growth. Continuously educate yourself and stay abreast of emerging trends. The more knowledge and skills you acquire, the better equipped you'll be to refine your goals and achieve them.

Finally, maintain a balanced life. Goal setting for financial success shouldn't come at the expense of your health and happiness. Strive for a life where financial goals coexist with personal well-being. This holistic approach ensures that when you do achieve financial freedom, you're healthy and happy enough to enjoy it.

With a solid foundation of well-defined goals, a practical plan of action, and continuous personal development, you're now well-equipped to tackle the journey ahead. The path to financial freedom is a marathon, not a sprint, requiring persistence, patience, and unwavering commitment. But with the right goals guiding you, the destination is well within your reach.

Understanding Your Financial Starting Point

Before diving headfirst into building streams of passive income, it's crucial to take a moment to understand your financial starting point. This introspective journey sets the stage for your financial roadmap and highlights where you stand today. Think of it as taking a snapshot of your current financial health.

First, conduct a thorough assessment of your assets and liabilities. Your assets might include savings accounts, retirement funds, real estate properties, and other investments. On the flip side, liabilities could encompass credit card debt, student loans, mortgages, and other financial obligations. Knowing where you stand helps you strategize effectively and set realistic financial goals.

Understanding your income and expenses is another critical step. Track your monthly income from all sources, such as your salary, freelance work, or side hustles. Equally essential is to document your monthly expenses, including bills, groceries, entertainment, and incidental expenditures. This balance sheet will help you identify areas where you can cut back and save more.

It's also important to examine your credit score and report. Your creditworthiness affects your ability to secure loans, finance investments, and even get favorable interest rates. Take the time to review your credit report for any discrepancies and work on improving your score if needed. A healthy credit score can open doors to more significant opportunities down the line.

Once you've painted a clear picture of your financial status, set some specific, measurable, achievable, relevant, and time-bound (SMART) financial goals. Whether it's saving for an emergency fund, paying off debt, or making a down payment on a rental property, these goals will guide your journey toward financial freedom. Start with short-term objectives that build a pathway to your long-term vision.

Understanding your financial starting point also means knowing your risk tolerance. Every investment has an associated risk, and it's crucial to determine how much risk you're willing to take. Are you more conservative, preferring safer, low-yield investments, or are you comfortable with higher risks for potentially greater rewards? Knowing this will help you tailor your investment strategy accordingly.

Next, look at your emergency savings. Financial experts often recommend having three to six months' worth of living expenses saved up. This buffer can provide peace of mind and security, allowing you to take calculated risks without jeopardizing your financial stability.

Financial literacy cannot be overstated. Equip yourself with knowledge by reading books, attending seminars, and following reputable finance blogs or podcasts. Understanding concepts like compound interest, asset diversification, and tax implications will empower you to make informed decisions as you build your passive income streams.

Also, take a moment to analyze your current lifestyle and spending habits. Are there areas where you can cut back and divert that money into investments or savings? Sometimes, small adjustments in your daily expenditures can make a significant difference over time.

If you're receiving any windfalls like bonuses, tax returns, or inheritance, think about how you can use these funds strategically. Rather than spending impulsively, use this extra capital to fund your passive income initiatives or pay off high-interest debts.

Consider your employment situation. Are you in a stable job with opportunities for growth, or is it time to think about a career change that aligns better with your financial goals? Sometimes, increasing your active income first is necessary before you can effectively transition to passive income streams.

Your financial circle is another vital aspect. Surround yourself with individuals who are financially savvy and have achieved goals similar to yours. Mentors, financial advisors, or peer groups can offer valuable insights, advice, and even accountability as you embark on this journey.

Also, keep a keen eye on the economic environment. Stay informed about trends, market conditions, and economic policies that could impact your financial strategies. Being proactive and adaptable to changes will help you navigate your financial journey more effectively.

Finally, don't underestimate the power of visualization and mindset. Envision where you want to be financially and allow that vision to guide your daily actions and decisions. Cultivate a positive and resilient mindset to overcome obstacles and stay focused on your goals.

Remember, understanding your financial starting point isn't a one-time event. Regularly revisit and update your financial assessment to ensure you're on track and make adjustments as needed. This continuous evaluation will keep you grounded and focused, setting a solid foundation for your financial future.

The Importance of Financial Literacy

Laying the foundation for a successful journey towards financial freedom starts with mastering the basics. And, at the heart of these basics, lies the indispensable skill of financial literacy. It's not just a buzzword; it's a life skill that can have a transformative impact on your journey toward building multiple streams of passive income.

Financial literacy, quite simply, is the ability to understand and effectively use various financial skills, including personal financial management, budgeting, and investing. This isn't about getting a degree in finance. It's about equipping yourself with the knowledge to make informed and effective decisions with your financial resources. Think of it as the bedrock upon which all your passive income endeavors will be built.

One of the first steps in achieving financial literacy is understanding your starting point. Know where your finances stand right now—an honest assessment of your income, expenses, debts, and savings. This might sound daunting, but it's crucial. Without knowing your starting point, it's like trying to navigate a ship without a map or compass. Clear financial records can highlight areas where you are overspending and reveal opportunities for savings, both of which are essential in freeing up capital for investment in passive income ventures.

Once you have a firm grasp on your financial situation, it's much easier to set realistic and achievable financial goals. Financial literacy empowers you to create SMART (Specific, Measurable, Achievable, Relevant, Time-bound) goals that will guide your journey. This strategic approach demystifies the path to financial independence, making it something tangible and attainable rather than a vague dream.

Understanding fundamental financial concepts like interest rates, inflation, and the time value of money can significantly impact your financial decisions. For instance, appreciating how compound interest works can transform your perspective on long-term savings and investments. The money you save and invest today can grow exponentially over time, but only if you make informed choices based on sound financial principles.

Investing is often intimidating for beginners, but financial literacy can break down these barriers. It helps you understand different types of investments, such as stocks, bonds, mutual funds, and real estate, each with its own set of risks and returns. This knowledge can demystify the investment process, allowing you to allocate your resources in a way that aligns with your risk tolerance and financial goals.

Moreover, financial literacy arms you with the knowledge to diversify your income sources. Understanding various income-generating assets not only spreads your risk but also maximizes your returns. This diversification is crucial in creating a robust passive income portfolio that can withstand market fluctuations and economic downturns.

Budgeting is another key component of financial literacy. A well-planned budget ensures that you're living within your means and setting aside funds for future investments. It involves tracking your income and expenditures to ensure you're not overspending. A disciplined approach to budgeting can free up resources, which you can channel into building your passive income streams.

Tax literacy is often overlooked but incredibly important. Knowing how different investments are taxed, what deductions are available, and how to file your taxes efficiently can save you a considerable amount of money each year. This savings can then be reinvested into your passive income projects, accelerating your path to financial independence.

Financial literacy also prepares you to deal with financial setbacks and emergencies. An emergency fund is a critical component of financial planning, providing a safety net that allows you to weather unexpected expenses without derailing your long-term financial goals. Knowing how to manage debt effectively, whether it's student loans, credit card debt, or mortgages, can also contribute to your financial well-being and peace of mind.

In the realm of passive income, financial literacy can help you discern legitimate opportunities from scams. The internet is full of get-rich-quick schemes that promise extraordinary returns with little effort. With a solid foundation in financial literacy, you're better equipped to identify and pursue genuine opportunities while avoiding potential pitfalls.

Moreover, financial literacy is a lifelong learning process. The financial landscape constantly evolves, with new investment vehicles, financial products, and economic conditions. Committing to continuous learning and staying informed about financial trends and policies can keep you ahead of the curve, ensuring you're always making the best possible decisions for your financial future.

Financial literacy also involves understanding legalities and compliance issues related to investments and income streams. Knowledge about legal structures, tax implications, and regulatory requirements can protect your assets and ensure that your financial affairs are in order, reducing the risk of legal complications down the line.

Another powerful benefit of financial literacy is the confidence it instills. When you understand how money works, making financial decisions becomes less intimidating. This confidence can drive you to take calculated risks necessary for achieving higher returns, helping you build and expand your passive income streams more effectively.

Finally, financial literacy isn't just about individual prosperity—it's also about empowering those around you. By mastering financial principles, you can share your knowledge with friends, family, and even your community, fostering a more financially literate society that supports mutual growth and success.

In conclusion, the importance of financial literacy cannot be overstated. It's the foundation upon which all your efforts to achieve financial freedom will rest. By investing time and effort into becoming financially literate, you're setting yourself up for long-term success and ensuring that your journey toward multiple streams of passive income will be as smooth and rewarding as possible.

Chapter 4:
Passive Income Through Real Estate

For those eager to escape the 9-to-5 grind and achieve financial freedom, real estate offers a robust path to generating passive income. Unlike many other investments, real estate provides the dual advantage of appreciating asset value and steady rental income. It's not just about buying a property; it involves meticulous planning, from picking the right location to securing financing under favorable terms. But don't worry, even if you're not interested in being a landlord, Real Estate Investment Trusts (REITs) offer a hands-off approach to investing in real estate. Additionally, platforms like Airbnb have revolutionized short-term rentals, making it simpler than ever to turn your home or investment property into a lucrative income stream. Each of these avenues requires a different level of involvement, but they all share a common goal: creating a steady flow of income that frees you from the constraints of traditional employment.

Getting Started with Rental Properties

Diving into rental properties is like opening the door to a wealth-building strategy that thrives on consistency and smart decision-making. Whether you're dreaming of a single rental unit or envisioning a portfolio of properties, the journey begins with understanding the basics. Start by identifying promising areas with growing demand—consider the classic real estate mantra: "location, location, location." Next, you'll need to assess your financing options.

Research loans, grants, and partnerships to leverage your purchasing power. Remember, your early investments set the tone for future success, so be mindful of cash flow, tenant management, and property maintenance. By thoroughly vetting potential properties and prioritizing tenant satisfaction, you're laying the groundwork for a reliable stream of passive income. Stay patient, stay informed, and most importantly, stay committed—your future financial freedom hinges on these initial, crucial steps.

Location, Location, Location—this isn't just a catchy phrase tossed around by seasoned real estate moguls; it's the cornerstone of successful rental property investments. To put it simply, the location of your property can be the make-or-break factor for your passive income stream. So why is it so critically important, you ask? Let's dig into that.

First off, the location of your property largely dictates the type of tenants you'll attract. You want to aim for areas with a strong job market, good schools, and low crime rates. Properties in such regions are high in demand, meaning you're more likely to find quality tenants who pay on time and take good care of your property. It's about creating a win-win situation for both you and your future tenants.

When evaluating a location, employment opportunities play a significant role. Areas near economic hubs offer stable job markets, which tend to attract long-term tenants. Think about it: tenants with stable jobs are less likely to move frequently, ensuring steady rental income for you. If you're considering a property, check local employment rates and the presence of large companies or industries.

School districts are another critical factor, especially if you're targeting family tenants. Good schools are often deal-makers for families. Properties in top-rated school districts usually have lower vacancy rates and higher rental prices. Check school ratings online or visit the schools yourself; you'll gain insights into the community's overall quality as well.

Don't overlook crime rates either. A high-crime area can be a significant deterrent for potential tenants. Use online resources to check crime statistics or talk to local law enforcement agencies. Remember, a safe neighborhood not only attracts tenants but also helps in appreciating your property's value over time.

Another aspect to consider is the lifestyle and amenities offered by a location. Areas near shopping centers, parks, public transportation, and entertainment options tend to be more desirable. These amenities add value to the living experience, making your property more attractive to prospective tenants. Therefore, property near amenities often supports higher rental rates and lower vacancy periods.

Look at the future development plans of the area as well. Future growth signals a potential increase in property values. If there are plans for new schools, hospitals, or commercial centers, you might see better returns on your investment. Areas on the brink of development can often be purchased at lower prices, setting you up for capital appreciation as the area grows.

Proximity to public transportation is also crucial. Easy access to buses, trains, and major roads can significantly influence a tenant's decision, particularly in urban areas. Properties close to transportation hubs generally see lower vacancy rates and can charge higher rents. After all, convenience is a big selling point.

Understanding local rent prices is essential. Overcharging can keep your property vacant, while undercharging can reduce your profit margins. Research similar properties in the area to get a sense of the going rates. Tools like rental market reports can provide insights into the average rent prices, helping you set a competitive yet profitable rate.

Naturally, you'll want to analyze the local supply and demand. If there's an oversupply of rental properties in your desired location, you might find it challenging to attract tenants. Conversely, a high demand with limited supply can allow you to command higher rents and experience shorter vacancy periods.

Don't forget about the legal landscape. Landlord-tenant laws can vary significantly across regions. Understanding the local regulations can save you a lot of headaches. For instance, some areas have stringent rent control laws, while others might be more landlord-friendly. Make sure you're familiar with the local laws to avoid any legal pitfalls.

An often overlooked but vital point is the cost of homeownership in the area. Property taxes, insurance rates, and homeowner association fees can vary dramatically. These costs will directly affect your return on investment (ROI). Running the numbers before making a purchase will give you a clearer picture of your potential profit margins.

Lastly, think about your management strategy. If you plan to manage the property yourself, proximity to your home can make a huge difference. Being nearby allows you to address issues quickly and efficiently. However, if your target location is far, hiring a property management firm might be a better option, albeit at a cost.

In conclusion, selecting the right location is about balancing these various factors to maximize your rental income and property value. A well-chosen location not only ensures a steady stream of quality tenants but also builds significant long-term equity. Location remains the bedrock upon which your rental property success is built, making it a non-negotiable aspect of any real estate investment strategy.

Financing Your First Property starts with understanding that securing the right financing can make or break your journey into real estate investment. You'll need smart strategies and perhaps a bit of hustle to secure funds, but the payoff can be immense. Financing is the lifeblood of your real estate venture, ensuring you can acquire properties that will generate passive income and help you escape the daily grind.

First off, let's discuss the importance of evaluating your financial health. Before you can even think about financing a property, you need a clear picture of your financial standing. This means pulling your credit report, assessing your debt-to-income ratio, and having a thorough understanding of your cash flow. Knowing your financial position allows you to make informed decisions and be prepared when approaching lenders.

One of the most common ways to finance your first property is through a traditional mortgage. This involves working with a bank or a financial institution to secure a loan. However, getting approved for a mortgage requires good credit, a reliable income stream, and a down payment, typically around 20% of the property's value. Remember, the better your credit score, the more favorable your terms will be.

For those who might not have a substantial down payment, there are options such as FHA loans. FHA loans are backed by the Federal Housing Administration and allow for lower down payments, sometimes as low as 3.5%. While these loans can make buying your first property more accessible, keep in mind they come with certain conditions and potential additional costs, like mortgage insurance.

Another option to consider is leveraging your existing assets. If you own a home, you can take out a home equity loan or a home equity line of credit (HELOC). This allows you to use the equity you've built in your current home to finance the down payment or even purchase a property outright. Be cautious, though; putting your primary residence on the line involves risk, so weigh the pros and cons carefully.

Private lenders and hard money loans are another avenue. These are generally short-term loans provided by individuals or companies.

They tend to have higher interest rates, but they also offer quicker approval processes and less stringent requirements than traditional banks. These can be beneficial if you're looking to flip properties or need quick funding. Make sure to do your due diligence and understand the terms before committing.

Seller financing can also be a viable route, particularly in a buyer's market. In this scenario, the seller acts as the lender, and you make mortgage payments directly to them. This arrangement can be beneficial if you have trouble securing traditional financing or need more flexibility. However, finding a seller willing to offer this type of financing can be challenging.

Another creative financing method involves partnerships. If you're lacking funds or experience, partnering with someone who has what you need can be an excellent solution. Pooling resources allows you to invest in properties you wouldn't be able to afford otherwise. Just make sure that your partnership terms and agreements are clearly defined to avoid conflicts down the line.

Once you've secured your financing, it's crucial to keep a close eye on your expenses and returns. Setting up a separate account for your rental income and expenses can help you monitor cash flow and ensure you're covering all your costs, such as maintenance, property management, and mortgage payments. Proper bookkeeping will make your financial life much easier.

Many new investors overlook the importance of having a contingency fund. Unexpected expenses are a part of property ownership – repairs, vacancies, and emergencies can and will arise. Setting aside at least three to six months' worth of expenses can provide a safety net that keeps you from dipping into your personal funds or jeopardizing your financial stability.

One can't ignore the power of negotiation. Whether you're dealing with lenders, sellers, or contractors, strong negotiation skills can save you thousands of dollars and improve your bottom line. Don't be afraid to negotiate terms, interest rates, or ask for discounts. Every dollar saved is a dollar earned towards your passive income goals.

Additionally, researching and understanding the various tax benefits associated with real estate investments can significantly impact your financial outcome. For instance, mortgage interest, property taxes, and depreciation are all tax-deductible. Working with a knowledgeable accountant who specializes in real estate can maximize your tax advantages and contribute to better profitability.

Networking is another critical component in your financing strategy. Building relationships with real estate agents, brokers, and fellow investors can open doors to opportunities and provide insights you might not find on your own. Networking can also lead to referrals for favorable financing options or even introduce you to potential partners or private lenders.

Lastly, never stop educating yourself. The real estate market is dynamic, and staying informed about market trends, financing options, and investment strategies will keep you ahead of the curve. Continue reading, take courses, attend seminars, and learn from others' experiences to refine your approach continually. Knowledge is power, especially in the world of real estate investment.

Embrace these financing strategies with confidence and determination. You're not just buying properties; you're investing in your future, building a path to financial independence, and creating a legacy. Your first property is the cornerstone of your passive income empire, and with the right financing plan, you're setting yourself up for long-term success and freedom.

REITs: A Hands-Off Real Estate Investment Strategy

Real Estate Investment Trusts, or REITs, offer a compelling opportunity for those looking to dive into real estate without the hassle of property management. Think of REITs as a way to have your cake and eat it too; you get all the perks of real estate investment with none of the headaches of being a landlord.

So, what exactly is a REIT? In the simplest terms, a REIT is a company that owns, operates, or finances income-producing real estate. These companies pool the capital of numerous investors, allowing each investor to earn dividends from real estate investments—without having to buy, manage, or finance any properties themselves.

One of the primary attractions of REITs is the hands-off approach. You don't have to worry about late-night maintenance calls, tenant complaints, or property taxes. Instead, professional managers and executives handle the day-to-day operations. This frees up your time to focus on other income streams or simply enjoy life's other offerings.

REITs come in various shapes and sizes, each focusing on different types of properties. Some invest in residential buildings, others in commercial real estate like shopping malls or office buildings, and some even specialize in niche markets like healthcare facilities or data centers. This variety enables you to diversify your portfolio by investing in different sectors within the real estate market.

Now, if you're seeking stable and consistent income, you'll be pleased to know that REITs are required by law to distribute at least 90% of their taxable income in the form of dividends to their shareholders. This makes them an attractive option for anyone looking to generate a steady stream of passive income.

Before jumping in, it's crucial to do your homework. Look at the performance history of the REITs you're interested in. Check their dividend payout history, the quality of their assets, and the expertise of their management team. Remember, not all REITs are created equal, and due diligence is key to making a sound investment.

When it comes to getting started, it's as easy as buying shares of a stock. Most REITs are publicly traded on major stock exchanges, so they can be purchased through a brokerage account. This makes them accessible to anyone looking to start small and gradually build their investment.

Let's talk about the financial benefits. REITs are designed to be a middle ground between stocks and bonds. While they offer the income potential of bonds through dividends, they also have the growth potential of stocks. This unique combination can add both income and value appreciation to your investment portfolio.

But what about the risks? Like any investment, REITs come with their own set of risks. Factors such as market conditions, property values, and interest rates can affect the performance of REITs. It's essential to understand these risks and how they compare to those of traditional real estate investing and other asset classes.

One way to mitigate some of these risks is through diversification. Don't put all your money into a single REIT. Instead, spread your investments across various REITs that focus on different types of properties and regions. This diversification can help balance out the performance and reduce the impact of any single underperforming asset.

Tax implications are another critical aspect to consider. Dividends from REITs are generally taxed as ordinary income, which may be higher than the capital gains tax rate. However, certain tax-advantaged accounts like IRAs can help mitigate some of these taxes, making it worthwhile to consult with a tax advisor to optimize your strategy.

In addition to traditional REITs, there are also REIT ETFs (Exchange-Traded Funds) that offer a diversified portfolio of different REITs in one fund. This can be a simple yet effective way to instantly diversify your real estate investments without having to pick individual REITs yourself.

The accessibility, transparency, and passive nature of REITs make them an excellent choice for those who want to enjoy the benefits of real estate investments without the time commitment and responsibility that come with owning physical properties.

Finally, remember that REITs are not a "get-rich-quick" scheme. They are a long-term investment, designed to provide steady, consistent income over time. Patience and a well-researched strategy can help turn REITs into a powerful component of your passive income portfolio, bringing you one step closer to financial freedom.

Embracing REITs as part of your financial strategy can truly amplify your journey towards generating sustainable passive income. With professional management taking care of the nitty-gritty details, your focus can remain on expanding other income streams and cultivating a fulfilling life beyond the 9-to-5 grind. Whether you're a seasoned investor or just starting, REITs offer a hands-off, lucrative avenue to achieve your financial aspirations.

Airbnb and Short-Term Rentals

Airbnb and short-term rentals offer a unique opportunity to dive into the world of passive income through real estate without the long-term commitment typically associated with traditional rental properties. With the rise of the sharing economy, platforms like Airbnb have made it easier than ever for property owners to monetize their spaces, whether it's a spare room, an entire house, or even a quirky treehouse.

One of the great advantages of short-term rentals is flexibility. You can choose when to list your property, allowing you to set blackout dates for personal use or maintenance. Unlike long-term tenants, your commitment to any given guest is usually just a few days, minimizing your risk and exposure to potential problematic renters.

The income potential can be significantly higher with short-term rentals compared to traditional leasing. Depending on your location and the desirability of your property, you can charge premium rates, especially during peak tourist seasons or local events. A property in a high-demand, tourist-friendly area can generate multiple times the income of a long-term rental.

Getting started with Airbnb and short-term rentals might seem daunting, but it doesn't have to be. One of the first steps is to research your local regulations and ensure you comply with any licensing, zoning laws, or tax obligations. Some cities have strict rules about short-term rentals, so understanding the legal landscape is crucial to avoid fines or other legal issues.

Next, you'll want to prepare your property to be guest-ready. This means more than just a quick clean-up. Think about the guest experience: will they have access to Wi-Fi, fresh linens, and a fully stocked kitchen? Investing in these little extras can lead to better reviews and higher occupancy rates. Remember, your goal is to create a five-star experience that makes guests want to come back or recommend your place to others.

Once your property is prepared, take high-quality photos. Visuals are incredibly important on platforms like Airbnb, as they offer the first impression to potential guests. Professional photos can make a significant difference in how often your listing gets booked. Capturing your property in the best light can justify higher pricing and elevate your property's appeal.

Pricing your rental can be tricky but crucial. Too high, and you may deter potential guests; too low, and you might not cover your costs. Utilize dynamic pricing tools or software to adjust your rates based on demand, seasonality, and competitor pricing. Many platforms, including Airbnb, offer built-in pricing suggestions based on local data, which can be incredibly helpful for newcomers.

Marketing your property goes beyond just listing it on Airbnb. Leverage social media, local tourist boards, and even collaboration with local businesses to promote your rental. Word-of-mouth and good reviews can quickly amplify your exposure. Moreover, engage with your guests through personalized messaging and quick, friendly responses to inquiries to build trust and encourage bookings.

One of the key strategies for successful property management is automation. Consider using property management software (PMS) that integrates with your listing platform. These tools can automate tasks like guest communication, bookings, and even cleaning schedules. Automation frees up your time and minimizes the chances of human error, ensuring a smooth experience for both you and your guests.

Additionally, cultivating a vigilant approach to property maintenance is vital. Regular inspections and prompt attention to repairs not only keep your property in top shape but also prevent negative reviews. A small investment in preventive maintenance can save you from costly repairs and ensure your property remains appealing.

Understanding your target audience can also maximize your profits. Whether your property is ideal for business travelers, families, or couples, tailoring your marketing efforts to attract your ideal guest can enhance your occupancy rates and profitability. Offering amenities and packages that appeal specifically to your target demographic can set your property apart from the competition.

As your short-term rental business grows, consider scaling by acquiring additional properties or diversifying the type of properties you offer. This could mean investing in properties in different locations or experimenting with unique, niche accommodations like tiny homes or glamping sites. Diversifying your portfolio can mitigate risk and ensure a more stable income stream.

However, with growth comes the challenge of management. Once you have multiple properties, you might find it beneficial to hire a property manager or management company. While this will cut into your profits, it can significantly alleviate the day-to-day management stress, enabling you to focus on expanding your portfolio or exploring other passive income streams.

It's also essential to keep an eye on market trends and adapt accordingly. The short-term rental market can be volatile, influenced by economic conditions, travel trends, and even technological advancements. Staying adaptable and proactively updating your strategy can help you stay competitive and maximize your income potential.

Finally, always remember the importance of guest feedback. Reviews can make or break a short-term rental business. Regularly solicit feedback, address any issues proactively, and make improvements based on what your guests appreciate or suggest. Consistent positive reviews lead to higher visibility on platforms and can exponentially grow your business.

Airbnb and short-term rentals can be a lucrative addition to your passive income portfolio. With strategic planning, attention to detail, and a commitment to providing excellent guest experiences, you can transform a simple property into a reliable income-generating asset while enjoying the flexibility and creativity that this endeavor offers.

Chapter 5:
Creating Digital Products

Harnessing the power of digital products is a game-changer for anyone looking to escape the nine-to-five grind and build sustainable passive income streams. Whether you're creating eBooks, online courses, software, or mobile applications, the digital realm offers limitless possibilities for monetization and scaling. The key to success lies in identifying a niche where your expertise can shine, crafting compelling content, and employing savvy marketing strategies to reach a global audience. Imagine the freedom of earning while you sleep—digital products make this a reality by allowing you to sell once and profit multiple times. It's all about leveraging your unique skills and knowledge to offer valuable solutions that people are willing to pay for, thereby setting the foundation for ongoing financial autonomy and long-term wealth.

Identifying Your Niche

So, you're excited about the idea of creating digital products to achieve financial freedom. But before you dive in, you have to get one crucial element right – identifying your niche. Think of it as the foundation upon which you'll build your empire. The more solid and well-defined your niche is, the sturdier your path to passive income will be.

First things first, what exactly is a niche? In simple terms, a niche is a specialized segment of the market for a particular kind of product or service. Instead of trying to appeal to everyone, you're focusing on a specific audience with specific needs and interests. This may sound limiting, but it's actually liberating. It allows you to become an expert in a focused area and serve your audience better than broad-spectrum competitors.

Think of it this way – would you rather be a big fish in a small pond or a small fish in a vast ocean? When you zero in on a niche, you set yourself up to dominate that particular market. You're not casting your net wide and hoping for the best; you're strategically positioning yourself to meet the specific needs of a well-defined audience. This makes marketing your products easier, more effective, and less costly.

Now, let's talk about how to find your niche. Start by looking inward. What are you passionate about? What are your strengths and skills? Passion alone isn't enough, but it's a fantastic place to start. When you're passionate about something, you're more likely to put in the time and effort needed to make your digital product a success.

Next, think about market demand. Passion is crucial, but if there's no demand for what you're offering, it won't matter how enthusiastic you are. Use tools like Google Trends, keyword research, and social media analytics to gauge interest in your area of focus. Look for patterns, spikes in interest, and gaps that you could fill with your expertise.

Consider existing competition as well. Some competition is a good sign – it indicates market demand. However, you don't want to dive into an overly saturated market unless you have a unique angle or superior offering. Find a balance. Look for a niche that has enough demand but isn't completely flooded with competitors.

One effective strategy is to combine aspects of different niches. For instance, instead of creating a general fitness app, why not focus on fitness for busy professionals or fitness routines using minimal equipment? This way, you're catering to a specific subset of the market and positioning yourself as the go-to expert in that area.

Validating your niche is a step you can't skip. Create a minimum viable product (MVP) or a pilot version to test the waters. This could be a simple eBook, a short online course, or any form of a digital product that requires minimal investment of time and resources. Use feedback from this initial offering to refine your niche and improve your product.

Always remember, your niche can evolve. The market changes, new trends emerge, and consumer preferences shift. Stay adaptable and be willing to pivot if necessary. What's important is having a clear starting point and a strong initial focus.

It's also worth noting that once you establish yourself in a particular niche, you can branch out into related areas. For example, if you've created a successful online course on digital marketing, you could consider adding courses on SEO, content marketing, or social media strategies – essentially, you're broadening your reach within your primary niche.

One powerful tool for niche identification is community engagement. Participate in forums, join social media groups, and engage in discussions related to your area of interest. Observe the questions people are asking, the problems they're facing, and the solutions they're seeking. This real-time interaction can provide invaluable insights into what your target audience truly needs.

You also need to consider your long-term vision. Your niche should align with your broader goals and values. This isn't just about making money; it's about creating sustainable income streams that allow you to live the life you desire. Picture where you want to be in five or ten years. Does this niche support that vision?

Your niche should also be scalable. What may start as a simple digital product could expand into a full-fledged brand. Ensure there's room for growth and that the niche isn't so narrow that it limits your potential.

Finally, be ready to commit. Identifying your niche isn't a one-time task; it's an ongoing process. Stay curious, keep learning, and continue to refine your focus as you gather more data and experience. A well-defined niche can be a powerful compass guiding you toward financial freedom and long-term success.

So, grab that niche and make it yours. The journey may have its challenges, but with a clear focus and unyielding determination, you'll find that creating digital products can be your golden ticket to escaping the 9-to-5 grind and achieving the financial independence you've always dreamed of.

eBooks and Online Courses

Creating eBooks and online courses stands as a powerful avenue for generating passive income by leveraging your expertise and passion into valuable digital products. Imagine distilling your knowledge into an insightful eBook or breaking down complex subjects into engaging online courses. This not only scales your ability to teach and inspire but also builds a consistent revenue stream as these products continue to sell over time. Crafting content that is both compelling and informative is crucial, and your unique voice and approach will set your offerings apart in a crowded market. Once the content is ready, effective marketing strategies will amplify your reach, drawing in a global audience eager to benefit from your insights. By capitalizing on the ever-growing demand for online learning and digital reading, you position yourself to achieve significant, sustained income while making a meaningful impact on others' lives. Don't underestimate the potential of your knowledge; when structured correctly, it can be a cornerstone of your financial independence journey.

Crafting Compelling Content is an art that, when mastered, can transform your digital products from mediocre to extraordinary. Whether you're crafting an eBook, developing an online course, or creating any other type of digital content, understanding the essential elements that make content compelling is key to your success. Let's dive into specifics that will make your work stand out in a crowded marketplace.

First and foremost, your content needs to provide value. Users engage with content that offers them a clear benefit or solves a particular problem. Therefore, the cornerstone of compelling content is an understanding of your target audience's needs and desires. Conduct thorough market research to identify their pain points and craft your material to offer actionable solutions. By focusing on what your audience wants, you move from creating generic content to producing tailored, impactful materials.

Another critical element is authenticity. In an era where consumers are bombarded with content, authenticity acts as a differentiator. Share personal stories or case studies that highlight real-world applications of your content. Authenticity builds trust, a key ingredient in converting casual readers into loyal followers. When people feel a genuine connection with you or find your experiences relatable, they are more likely to engage with your content and invest in your offerings.

Tone and style matter immensely in capturing and retaining your audience's attention. Find a voice that resonates with your target market. The tone should align with the nature of your content and the expectations of your audience. Whether it's formal, casual, humorous, or informative, consistency is crucial. Inconsistencies can confuse readers and weaken your message. Use engaging language, avoid jargon unless it's industry-specific and necessary, and keep your writing as clear and concise as possible.

The structure of your content also plays a pivotal role. People today skim rather than read. Break your content into digestible chunks with subheadings, bullet points, and visuals where appropriate. This approach not only makes information easier to absorb but also keeps the reader engaged for longer. Each section should logically flow to the next, guiding the reader through your material seamlessly.

Engaging introductions and compelling conclusions are critical in crafting memorable content. Start with a hook—something that captures attention immediately, be it a startling fact, an intriguing question, or a bold statement. Your conclusion should reinforce the key takeaways and include a strong call-to-action (CTA). Whether it's encouraging readers to take a specific step, purchase a product, or simply reflect on the content, a powerful CTA can drive the action you want them to take.

Visual elements significantly enhance textual content. Incorporate images, infographics, and videos to complement and reinforce your message. Visuals not only break the monotony of text but also help explain complex concepts more clearly. The right visuals can improve comprehension and retention, making your content more impactful.

Storytelling is another powerful technique for making your content compelling. Stories captivate because they are innately human; they evoke emotions and create connections. Weave narratives into your content to illustrate your points, making the information more relatable and memorable. Whether it's a personal anecdote or a customer success story, storytelling can elevate your content from mundane to memorable.

Crafting compelling content also requires paying attention to details, particularly grammar and syntax. Poorly written content can distract from your message and diminish your credibility. Utilize tools such as grammar checkers and take the time to review and revise your work meticulously. A polished piece showcases professionalism and respect for your audience.

Engagement doesn't stop at content creation. Interaction with your audience is essential for making your content more compelling. Encourage reader feedback, questions, and discussions. Creating a dialogue around your content not only enhances engagement but also provides you with valuable insights into your audience's thoughts and concerns. This feedback loop can help you tailor future content to better serve your readers.

When crafting digital products such as eBooks or online courses, focus on organization. Plan your content structure before diving into writing. Create outlines and draft key points to ensure a logical flow of information. This preparation prevents your content from feeling disjointed and ensures a cohesive learning experience for your audience.

One often overlooked yet vital aspect of compelling content is updating it regularly. Information can become outdated, leading to a decline in relevance and value. Make it a habitual process to review and update your content to keep it fresh and accurate. Staying current not only maintains the utility of your material but also portrays you as an active, knowledgeable authority in your field.

In addition to text, leverage supplementary materials to augment the core content of your digital products. Downloadable resources, quizzes, and interactive elements can enrich the user experience. These additions provide added value and can help reinforce learning or understanding of key concepts.

Marketing your content is equally important as its creation. High-quality, compelling content serves no purpose if it remains unseen. Employ a strategic marketing plan to reach your target audience. Utilize social media platforms, email marketing, and search engine optimization (SEO) techniques to broaden your content's reach and impact.

In sum, **Crafting Compelling Content** is about striking a balance between value, authenticity, and engagement. By understanding your audience's needs, employing effective storytelling, maintaining a consistent tone, and ensuring impeccable detail, you place yourself in a position to create content that resonates. Remember, the goal is not just to attract an audience but to engage and retain them, turning them into loyal followers and, ultimately, customers.

Marketing Your Digital Products is where the magic happens—where your brilliant ideas get the recognition they deserve. You've put blood, sweat, and tears into creating top-notch digital products. Now, it's time to make sure the world knows about them. No matter how amazing your eBooks, online courses, or software applications are, they won't generate income if nobody buys them. Marketing is your golden ticket to transforming creations into cash flow.

First off, know your audience. Understanding who your ideal customers are will guide every aspect of your marketing strategy. Research demographics, psychographics, and buying behaviors. The more detailed your customer persona, the more effectively you can tailor your message. For instance, if you're selling an online course on digital painting, aim your efforts at aspiring artists, hobbyists, and potentially other educational institutions.

Next, build a stunning landing page. Your landing page serves as the digital handshake for your products. It should be visually appealing, easy to navigate, and packed with compelling copy that highlights the benefits your product offers. Don't forget to include powerful calls to action (CTAs) that urge visitors to make a purchase or sign up for more information.

Never underestimate the power of social media. Platforms like Facebook, Instagram, Twitter, and LinkedIn can be goldmines for driving traffic to your products. Create engaging posts, share snippets of your content, and use targeted ads to reach a broader audience. Utilize features like Facebook Groups or Instagram Stories to generate buzz and foster community engagement.

Leverage email marketing to keep potential customers in the loop. Collect email addresses through your website and social media channels by offering valuable lead magnets like free eBooks or trial subscriptions. Once you've built a list, send out regular newsletters that provide useful content, updates on new products, and special promotions. The goal is to nurture leads into long-term customers.

Collaborate with influencers and affiliates to expand your reach. Identify key influencers in your niche and negotiate partnerships that allow them to promote your products to their followers. Similarly, setting up an affiliate program can incentivize others to market your products, offering them a commission for each sale they generate. Both strategies can significantly boost your exposure with relatively low effort on your part.

Offer limited-time discounts and special promotions. Everyone loves a good deal, and a sense of urgency can prompt quick decisions. Holiday specials, flash sales, and exclusive early-bird pricing are effective tactics. Just ensure that your messages are consistent across all marketing channels to avoid confusion.

Don't overlook the power of content marketing. Publishing blog posts, videos, podcasts, and webinars related to your expertise can attract organic traffic to your website. When people find value in the content you offer for free, they're more likely to invest in your paid products. It's all about building trust and establishing yourself as an authority in your field.

Invest in search engine optimization (SEO) to ensure your products show up in relevant searches. Conduct keyword research to understand what terms and phrases your potential customers are using. Incorporate these keywords naturally into your website content, blog posts, and product descriptions. Higher search engine rankings can lead to increased visibility and, ultimately, more sales.

Use analytics to track your marketing performance. Tools like Google Analytics can provide valuable insights into what's working and what's not. Monitor metrics like traffic sources, bounce rates, and conversion rates. This data will help you fine-tune your strategies and allocate resources more effectively.

Customer reviews and testimonials can be incredibly persuasive. Ask satisfied customers to leave positive reviews or provide testimonials you can feature on your landing page and in marketing materials. Real-life success stories lend credibility and can sway hesitant buyers.

Engage in A/B testing to optimize your efforts further. Experiment with different headlines, images, CTAs, and promotional offers to see what resonates most with your audience. Small tweaks can sometimes lead to significant improvements in conversion rates.

Don't be afraid to think outside the box and try unconventional marketing techniques. Guerilla marketing, viral campaigns, or even a well-placed PR stunt can create massive buzz around your product. The key is to ensure these efforts align with your brand and appeal to your target audience.

Constantly update and improve your products based on customer feedback. Listening to your customers not only helps you refine your offerings but also shows that you value their input, fostering loyalty and encouraging repeat business. Happy customers are your best marketing asset.

Finally, embrace continuous learning. The digital marketing landscape is ever-changing, with new tools, tactics, and trends emerging regularly. Stay updated with industry news, attend webinars, and consider enrolling in digital marketing courses. The more you know, the better you can adapt and stay ahead of the competition.

Remember, marketing is not a one-time effort but an ongoing process. By consistently applying these strategies, you'll not only increase your sales but also build a loyal customer base that will support you as you grow. So, gear up, take action, and witness your digital products soar to new heights.

Software and Mobile Applications

If there's one area in digital products that offers tremendous potential for passive income, it's software and mobile applications. Think about it: these applications solve specific problems, entertain, educate, or provide convenience to millions of users daily. The digital landscape is continually evolving, and the demand for innovative software solutions is skyrocketing.

Creating a software application might sound intimidating, especially if you're not a programmer. But don't worry—you don't need to be a tech guru to dive into this realm. Many successful entrepreneurs have built thriving software businesses without writing a single line of code. Thanks to various tools, platforms, and outsourcing options, the barriers to entry are lower than ever before.

The first step in creating a successful software or mobile application is identifying a problem that needs solving. Look around at the daily challenges people face in different niches: finance, health, education, entertainment, productivity, and more. The goal is to pinpoint a pain point and design a solution. Your app could be as straightforward as a budgeting tool or as complex as a fitness tracking platform.

Validation is crucial before pouring resources into development. Share your idea with potential users, collect feedback, and assess the demand. This step will save you time and money by ensuring there is a market for your product. Use social media, forums, and surveys to gauge interest and get honest feedback about your concept.

Once you've validated your idea, it's time to bring it to life. If you're tech-savvy, you might choose to build the app yourself. There are numerous programming languages and frameworks at your disposal, such as Swift for iOS or Kotlin for Android. The key here is selecting the right tool that aligns with your skillset and the app's requirements.

For those who aren't keen on coding, no-code and low-code platforms like Bubble or Appgyver offer user-friendly interfaces to develop applications. These platforms enable you to drag and drop elements, automate workflows, and eventually deploy your app without delving into complex programming languages.

If the DIY route still seems daunting, consider outsourcing the development work. You can hire freelance developers through platforms like Upwork or Toptal. When outsourcing, it's imperative to communicate your vision clearly and ensure that the developers grasp the functionality and user experience you envision.

With a working prototype or MVP (Minimum Viable Product) in hand, begin testing it rigorously. Beta testing with a small group of users can help uncover any glitches, usability issues, and areas for improvement. Feedback from this phase is invaluable—it's your chance to refine and perfect the app before a broader release.

Monetization strategies for software and mobile applications are diverse. You could adopt a freemium model, where basic features are free, and users pay for premium options. Subscription models are another lucrative option, offering recurring revenue as users pay monthly or yearly fees for continuous access to your app. Alternatively, you can charge a one-time fee for download or include in-app purchases to enhance user experience.

Marketing your application is equally crucial. Even the most groundbreaking app will languish if no one knows about it. Utilize SEO techniques to ensure your app appears in relevant search results. Leverage social media, app review sites, and influencer partnerships to build buzz and attract downloads. Investing in a robust marketing strategy will amplify your reach and expedite user acquisition.

Post-launch, continuous updates and improvements are critical for retaining users and remaining competitive. Listen to user feedback and roll out updates that address concerns and add new features. An engaged user base is more likely to stay loyal and recommend your app to others, creating a cycle of growth and sustainability.

Analyzing user behavior through analytics tools can provide insights into how your app is being used and what drives user retention. Understanding patterns and preferences allows you to make data-driven decisions that enhance user satisfaction. Remember, the ultimate goal is to keep users hooked and returning for more.

Finally, don't underestimate the power of customer support. Providing excellent support can turn a frustrated user into a loyal advocate. Whether it's through chatbots, email, or in-app help, ensuring users feel heard and assisted can significantly impact your app's reputation and success.

In conclusion, software and mobile applications represent a golden opportunity for generating passive income. The key is to identify a problem, validate your idea, execute thoughtfully, market effectively, and continually iterate based on user feedback. By approaching this venture methodically and creatively, you can establish a steady stream of income that supports your journey to financial freedom.

Chapter 6:
Stock Market Investing for Passive Income

Diving into the stock market can be an excellent way to generate passive income, given the right strategies. By understanding dividends, you can appreciate how companies distribute a portion of their earnings to shareholders, providing a steady cash flow. Building a dividend portfolio involves selecting stocks from financially sound companies with a history of regular and increasing dividend payouts. Besides individual stocks, Exchange-Traded Funds (ETFs) and mutual funds play a crucial role. They offer diversified investment options that can reduce risk while ensuring a more stable income stream. The beauty of stock market investing for passive income lies in its scalability and potential for long-term growth, making it a powerful component of your financial freedom toolkit.

Understanding Dividends

When it comes to creating passive income through the stock market, dividends play a crucial role. Dividends are the regular payouts companies make to their shareholders, and understanding how they work can significantly enhance your financial strategy. At its core, investing in dividend-paying stocks means you're investing in businesses that share a portion of their profits with you, the shareholder. This act of sharing profit is what generates a stream of passive income that can support your financial independence journey.

So, how exactly do dividends work? When a company earns profits, management has a few choices: reinvest the profits back into the company, pay off debt, buy back shares, or distribute a portion of the earnings to shareholders in the form of dividends. Companies that opt to distribute dividends often have stable, mature businesses with consistent profitability. These businesses view dividend distributions as a way to reward shareholders and retain investor loyalty.

To receive dividends, you need to own shares of a company before the ex-dividend date. The ex-dividend date is the cut-off day that determines who qualifies for the dividend payout. If you buy a stock on or after this date, you won't receive the next dividend payment. Dividends are typically paid quarterly, although some companies pay them monthly or annually.

The appeal of dividend investing lies in its dual benefit. First, you earn a regular income without having to sell any of your investments. Second, if you reinvest your dividends (a strategy known as dividend reinvestment), you can increase your holdings and potentially enhance your returns through the power of compounding. This reinvestment approach often leads to more shares, which in turn generate more dividends, creating a snowball effect of wealth accumulation.

However, not all dividends are created equal, and it's essential to analyze the sustainability of a company's dividend. One way to assess sustainability is by looking at the dividend payout ratio—the percentage of earnings a company pays out as dividends. A high payout ratio might indicate that a company is distributing most of its earnings, which could be unsustainable if profits decline. Conversely, a lower payout ratio suggests the company has room to grow its dividends.

Another crucial metric is the dividend yield, which is the annual dividend payment divided by the stock's current price. While a high dividend yield might seem attractive, it's often worth investigating further. Sometimes, an unusually high yield can signal underlying issues with the company, such as declining stock prices or financial instability. Striking a balance between yield and sustainability is key to building a robust dividend portfolio.

Moreover, it's important to consider the company's history of dividend payments. Businesses with a strong track record of maintaining or increasing dividends over the years tend to be more reliable. Such dividend aristocrats, companies that have increased their dividends annually for at least 25 consecutive years, are often stalwarts of stability and financial strength. Investing in these companies can provide a dependable stream of passive income.

Market sectors also play a role in dividend investing. Traditional dividend-paying sectors include utilities, real estate, and consumer staples. These sectors often generate consistent cash flows, enabling them to pay regular dividends. However, diversification across various sectors can protect your portfolio from industry-specific risks and ensure a more stable dividend income.

One aspect often overlooked is the tax implications of dividends. Dividend income can be taxed at different rates depending on whether it's classified as qualified or ordinary dividends. Qualified dividends, typically from U.S. companies and held for a specific period, enjoy lower tax rates, whereas ordinary dividends are taxed at your regular income tax rate. Understanding these distinctions helps in planning your taxes and maximizing after-tax returns.

Next, let's talk about the mechanics of getting started with dividend investing. Begin by identifying companies with solid financial health, stable earnings, and a history of dividend payments. Research their payout ratios, dividend yields, and overall industry health. Tools like financial news outlets, stock screener platforms, and analyst reports can provide valuable insights to help you make informed decisions.

It's also beneficial to tap into resources like dividend-focused ETFs (Exchange-Traded Funds) or mutual funds. These funds invest in a diversified basket of dividend-paying stocks, offering exposure to various companies and sectors without needing to pick stocks individually. This can simplify the investment process and provide instant diversification.

Building a dividend portfolio is not an overnight task. It requires time, patience, and ongoing evaluation. Regularly monitor your portfolio to ensure the companies continue to perform well and meet your dividend expectations. Reinvest any dividends you receive to compound your returns further and adjust your holdings if a company cuts its dividend or shows signs of financial distress.

Lastly, let's acknowledge the emotional and psychological facets of dividend investing. Holding onto dividend stocks can teach patience, especially since success doesn't come overnight. As the dividends roll in, they can offer a sense of financial security and gradual progress towards your passive income goals. This steady income stream can provide peace of mind, knowing you're drawing a step closer to financial freedom.

In summary, understanding dividends and how they fit into your passive income strategy is vital. By carefully selecting dividend-paying stocks, monitoring your portfolio, and reinvesting your earnings, you can build a reliable income stream that supports your journey to financial freedom. Dividends offer a powerful way to make your money work for you, one payout at a time. So, take the knowledge you've gained here and make dividends a cornerstone of your passive income plan.

Building a Dividend Portfolio

You've heard the saying, "Don't put all your eggs in one basket." When it comes to passive income through stock market investing, building a diversified dividend portfolio is the embodiment of that wisdom. The idea is to create a steady, reliable stream of income by investing in companies that pay out a portion of their earnings as dividends to shareholders.

The first step in building a dividend portfolio is understanding the types of companies that typically pay dividends. Generally, these are established businesses with stable cash flows and a long history of profitability. Think of companies in sectors like utilities, consumer staples, and healthcare. These industries tend to be less volatile and more consistent in their performance, making them reliable sources of dividend income.

Once you've identified the sectors you're interested in, it's time to research specific companies. Look for those with a strong track record of paying and increasing dividends over time. This history is often an indicator of a company's financial health and commitment to returning value to shareholders. Key metrics to consider include the dividend yield, payout ratio, and the company's earnings growth.

Dividend yield is a critical metric—and it couldn't be easier to calculate. Simply divide the annual dividend payment by the stock's current price. A higher yield often attracts investors, but be cautious; an unusually high yield could be a red flag indicating an underlying issue with the company. Aim for a balance—companies that offer decent yields but are also financially stable.

Next, focus on the payout ratio. This ratio measures the percentage of earnings a company pays out as dividends. A lower payout ratio could mean the company is reinvesting more into growth opportunities, but it also provides a cushion for maintaining dividends during tough times. Typically, a payout ratio below 60% is considered healthy.

When choosing companies, look for dividend aristocrats—companies that have a history of increasing their dividends for at least 25 consecutive years. These firms have shown resilience through various economic cycles and are likely to continue growing their payouts. Examples include blue-chip giants like Procter & Gamble and Johnson & Johnson.

Once you've selected your investments, diversification across different sectors is crucial. While it might be tempting to load up on high-yield stocks from a single industry, this practice exposes your portfolio to sector-specific risks. By spreading your investments across various industries, you mitigate these risks and enhance the stability of your income stream.

Another important aspect is geographical diversification. Don't limit yourself to domestic stocks. Many foreign companies offer attractive dividends, and investing internationally can further reduce your risk. Be mindful of foreign tax implications, but the added layer of diversity often outweighs these concerns.

Reinvesting dividends through a Dividend Reinvestment Plan (DRIP) can amplify the growth of your portfolio. DRIPs allow you to use your dividend payouts to purchase additional shares of the company, often without brokerage fees. This compounding effect can significantly boost your investment over time.

It's tempting to chase high yields, especially when starting. However, prioritize quality over quantity. High-yielding stocks are often in cyclical industries and can face steep cuts during downturns. A balanced portfolio, combining both high and moderate yielders from various sectors, tends to be more resilient.

Monitoring your dividend portfolio is crucial. Keep an eye on company earnings reports, dividend announcements, and market conditions. While the goal is passive income, you can't adopt a "set it and forget it" mentality completely. Periodic reviews ensure you make necessary adjustments to maintain your portfolio's health.

Incorporating exchange-traded funds (ETFs) or mutual funds into your portfolio can also provide diversification and professional management. Dividend-focused ETFs or mutual funds can give you exposure to a broad range of dividend-paying stocks with one purchase, simplifying the diversification process.

Remember that patience is key when building a dividend portfolio. The real magic happens through compounding over time. It might take years to see significant income, but the stability and reliability make it worth the wait. This is not a get-rich-quick strategy; it's a build-wealth-slowly-but-surely approach.

Lastly, pay attention to taxes. Dividends are taxable income, and knowing your tax bracket will help you plan better. Qualified dividends are usually taxed at a lower rate compared to ordinary income, but always consult a tax advisor to optimize your strategy.

Building a dividend portfolio requires careful planning, ongoing management, and a long-term perspective. Yet, the potential for reliable, growing passive income makes it an invaluable component of your financial independence journey. Start small, stay informed, and watch your dividends grow into a robust income stream.

The Role of ETFs and Mutual Funds

When it comes to stock market investing for passive income, both Exchange-Traded Funds (ETFs) and mutual funds hold a significant role. They're often touted as the bedrock for long-term, hands-off investing. But what makes them so indispensable for those looking to break free from the nine-to-five grind and achieve financial freedom? Let's dive into it.

First off, both ETFs and mutual funds provide a unique opportunity for diversification. Diversification is a critical aspect of investing because it spreads your risk across various assets, reducing the impact of any single investment's poor performance. Imagine you've got a portfolio, and one stock takes a nosedive—if you've diversified, the blow to your overall portfolio is cushioned. This becomes particularly appealing when your goal is to generate consistent, passive income over time.

One of the standout features of ETFs is their flexibility. Unlike mutual funds, which can only be bought or sold at the end of the trading day, ETFs trade like individual stocks. This means you can buy and sell ETFs anytime the market is open, giving you more control and liquidity. If you see an opportunity or need to reallocate funds quickly, ETFs make this process straightforward.

Mutual funds, on the other hand, offer a robust structure managed by professional fund managers. This can be a blessing for those who don't have the time, expertise, or inclination to manage their investments actively. The fund managers take care of the buying, selling, and overall strategy, allowing you to benefit from their expertise while enjoying your passive earnings.

Management style plays a crucial role in distinguishing between mutual funds and ETFs. Many mutual funds are actively managed, meaning a professional manager or a team makes decisions about how to allocate assets. While this can result in higher fees, the aim is to outperform the market. Conversely, most ETFs are passively managed, tracking specific indices. This usually translates to lower fees, making them a cost-effective choice for long-term investors.

Now, let's talk about dividends, a cornerstone of passive income. Both ETFs and mutual funds can be structured to provide regular dividend payments. These payouts can be reinvested to buy more shares or taken as cash, providing a steady income stream. If you're aiming for financial independence, these dividends can be powerful allies in building up your cash flow.

But how do you choose between ETFs and mutual funds? One key factor is your investment timeline. For those with a long-term horizon, mutual funds can offer consistent growth and the benefit of professional management. ETFs, with their lower fees and greater flexibility, might be better if you prefer a more hands-on approach or need access to your funds more readily.

Cost is another consideration. While mutual funds often come with higher expense ratios due to active management, they may justify these fees with better performance. On the flip side, ETFs generally have lower expense ratios, which can make a significant difference over the long term, especially when compounded returns are at play.

Another crucial aspect is the ease of access. Mutual funds are often sold through financial advisors or directly by the fund companies. ETFs can be bought through any brokerage account, making them more accessible for the average investor. This ease of access aligns well with the goal of creating sustainable passive income—they're simple, straightforward, and don't require a deep dive into complex financial products.

Tax efficiency is also worth noting. ETFs typically offer more tax advantages compared to mutual funds. Due to their unique structure, ETFs experience fewer taxable events. This can be particularly beneficial for minimizing capital gains taxes and maximizing your net returns, thus boosting your passive income.

So, why should you consider adding ETFs or mutual funds to your passive income strategy? The answer lies in their ability to provide steady, predictable returns with minimal effort on your part. By leveraging these investment vehicles, you're essentially putting your money to work for you, allowing you to focus on other income streams or simply enjoying the freedom you've worked so hard to achieve.

Moreover, ETFs and mutual funds allow for a balanced portfolio. Whether you're seeking growth, income, or a combination of both, there's likely a fund that matches your investment goals. This flexibility is invaluable for designing a portfolio tailored to your financial needs and long-term objectives.

The beauty of these funds is also in their automatic diversification. With one purchase, you're buying into a basket of assets, spreading risk, and reducing the volatility typically associated with individual stocks. This aligns perfectly with the ethos of passive income—steady, reliable, and requiring minimal active management.

To summarize, integrating ETFs and mutual funds into your passive income strategy can be a game-changer. They provide a means to achieve diversification, professional management, flexibility, and cost efficiency. These elements combined make them an essential tool for anyone serious about escaping the grind and attaining financial freedom.

As with any investment, the key is to conduct thorough research and consider your financial goals, risk tolerance, and timeline. With the right approach, ETFs and mutual funds can form a solid cornerstone of your passive income strategy, leading you one step closer to the financial independence you dream of.

Chapter 7:
Affiliate Marketing Mastery

Affiliate marketing is one of the most accessible and scalable ways to create a passive income stream, making it a perfect avenue for those looking to escape the 9-to-5 grind. You'll want to start by selecting profitable niches that align with your interests and expertise, ensuring you stay motivated and authentic. Building an affiliate website is essential; it serves as your main platform for attracting and engaging an audience. Focus on creating high-quality content that drives traffic through valuable information and insights. Incorporate SEO basics to boost visibility and organic reach, ensuring your site stands out in the crowded online marketplace. Remember, mastering affiliate marketing involves persistence, strategic planning, and the ability to pivot as needed to optimize and scale your efforts. When done right, it can pave the way to significant financial freedom.

Selecting Profitable Niches

When diving into affiliate marketing, the first and arguably one of the most crucial steps is selecting a niche. This choice can make or break your affiliate marketing endeavor. Understanding the significance of a niche is essential; it sets the direction of your entire business, impacting everything from content creation to target audience and even the affiliate products you'll promote.

What exactly constitutes a "profitable" niche? Simply put, it's a specialized segment of the market with high demand and an engaged audience willing to spend money. Yet, finding this golden opportunity isn't as straightforward as it might sound. To navigate the vast ocean of possibilities, you'll need a blend of strategic thinking, market research, and a bit of intuition.

Start by examining your interests and passions. While profitability is the ultimate goal, entering a niche you're genuinely interested in makes the journey more enjoyable and sustainable. Authenticity resonates with audiences; if you're passionate about your niche, it shows. This enthusiasm translates into better engagement, stronger relationships, and ultimately, higher conversions.

Next, consider the market demand. No matter how passionate you are about a topic, if there's little to no demand, your efforts might go unnoticed. Utilize tools like Google Trends, Keyword Planner, and various market research reports to gauge the popularity and search volume of potential niches. Look for trends and data points that signal steady or growing interest.

Competitor analysis is another key element. Examine existing players in your potential niche. Are there established websites and influencers? How saturated is the market? While a heavily saturated niche might indicate high demand, it also means more competition. A balance is needed here; you want enough competition to confirm demand but not so much that you're unable to carve out your own space.

Consider the profitability of your niche. Beyond just demand, think about the monetization potential. Are there high-quality products available for promotion? What's the commission structure like? Some niches offer higher commission rates but might have fewer products, while others might have abundant product options but lower payouts. Align this with your financial goals to make an informed decision.

A crucial yet often overlooked factor is the customer value. Not all niches have the same customer lifetime value (CLV). High-ticket items or niches with repeat purchase potential are goldmines in affiliate marketing. For instance, the health and wellness sector may offer recurring commissions through subscription-based products, whereas one-off purchases in some tech niches might not. A higher CLV means more revenue potential from each customer you acquire.

Some niches lend themselves better to high-quality content than others. Content-rich niches offer endless opportunities for blog posts, videos, reviews, and tutorials. Think about how much content you can realistically create and how it will fit within the overall strategy. Niches that allow for diversified content formats can enable you to capture a wider audience through different channels like YouTube, blogs, and social media.

Your niche should also align with long-term market trends. The last thing you want is to invest significant time and effort into a niche that's here today but gone tomorrow. Stable or growing niches are your safest bet. Look for evergreen topics, meaning those that remain relevant over time. Some great examples include personal finance, health, and fitness, and self-improvement.

Community and engagement levels can't be ignored. Niches with active and passionate communities often provide a vibrant ecosystem where your content and recommendations can thrive. Forums, social media groups, and online communities offer opportunities for networking, collaboration, and an engaged audience eager for your insights.

Don't forget to assess the SEO potential within your niche. Search engine optimization is a cornerstone for driving organic traffic, crucial for passive income streams. Investigate the keywords pertinent to your niche. How competitive are they? Are there long-tail keywords within the niche that you can target more easily? Your ability to rank well in search engines can greatly enhance the visibility and profitability of your affiliate site.

Also, remember to factor in your unique selling proposition (USP). What makes you stand out in your chosen niche? Having a USP differentiates you from the competition and builds your brand identity. It could be your unique voice, a different angle on common topics, or exclusive information and insights.

Before committing, test the waters. Start small. Create some content or even a mini website centered around your prospective niche and gauge the response. Monitor engagement metrics and feedback. This trial phase can provide invaluable insights and either validate your choice or signal a need to pivot.

Arming yourself with these tactics ensures you make an informed, strategic decision in niche selection. It's this calculated approach that separates the hobbyists from the successful, full-time affiliate marketers. Your chosen niche is not just a segment of the market; it's the foundation of your future in affiliate marketing. With due diligence, passion, and strategic thinking, you can carve out a profitable space and turn it into a sustainable stream of passive income.

Building an Affiliate Website

Creating a lucrative affiliate website is a cornerstone of affiliate marketing success and an essential pathway to financial independence. It starts with selecting a domain name that resonates with your chosen niche, reflecting both relevance and professionalism. Don't skimp on design – a clean, intuitive layout matters as much to your visitors as it does to your conversion rates. Quality content is your ticket to organic traffic; focus on producing informative, engaging posts that solve your audience's problems and subtly weave in affiliate links. Mastering basic SEO techniques ensures your content gets the visibility it deserves. Think strategically about monetization by integrating high-converting affiliate products and continually testing which offerings resonate most with your audience. Your goal is to create a website that not only attracts but retains visitors, turning casual browsers into loyal customers, thereby generating steady streams of passive income.

Content Creation for Traffic is the lifeblood of any successful affiliate marketing strategy. You could have the best products in the most lucrative niche but without traffic, you won't see a dime. Generating traffic isn't just about getting people to click on your links – it's about drawing the right audience and converting them into long-term followers and, ultimately, buyers. It's about consistency, quality, and understanding what your audience wants.

So, let's dive right in. The first step towards effective content creation is understanding your target audience. Who are they? What are their interests, needs, and pain points? The more you understand your audience, the more tailored and relevant your content will be. Use tools like Google Analytics, social media insights, and audience surveys to gather data. Once you know your audience, you can create content that speaks directly to them.

But just knowing your audience isn't enough. You need to craft value-rich content that stands out in a crowded digital landscape. High-quality content takes many forms including blog posts, videos, infographics, and podcasts. Each format has its advantages and is suitable for different types of information. Blog posts are great for in-depth guides and tutorials, while videos can capture the attention for product reviews and demonstrations.

Whatever format you choose, ensure your content is actionable and provides immediate value. People won't stick around if your content is fluff. Break down complex ideas into simple, digestible pieces. Include step-by-step guides, examples, and practical tips to help your audience solve their problems. Always focus on delivering value because value builds trust, and trust drives traffic.

SEO Basics are critical in ensuring your content reaches a broader audience through search engines. SEO, or Search Engine Optimization, is a set of strategies used to increase your website's visibility on search engines like Google. Start with keyword research to identify the terms your audience is searching for. Use tools like SEMrush or Ahrefs to find relevant keywords with a good balance between search volume and competition.

Incorporate these keywords naturally into your content, including headers, subheaders, and within the body text. Don't overstuff them, though. SEO is not only about keywords; it's about creating content that satisfies user intent. Make sure the content answers the questions or solves the problems indicated by those search terms.

Meta descriptions, alt text for images, and internal linking are additional SEO tactics to boost your visibility. A well-crafted meta description can improve your click-through rate (CTR) directly from the search results. Alt text helps search engines understand your images and is crucial for accessibility. Internal linking keeps visitors on your site longer and helps distribute page authority across your website.

Building Authority with your content is another pillar of driving traffic. When you're viewed as an authority in your niche, people are more likely to seek out and trust your content. To build this authority, consistently provide high-quality, reliable content. Case studies, expert interviews, and long-form guides can showcase your depth of knowledge. Also, guest posting on established blogs and participating in industry forums can enhance your credibility.

Social proof is an important aspect of authority. Testimonials, user reviews, and case studies from people who've benefited from your content or affiliate products can strongly influence new visitors. Don't be shy about showcasing these on your site. Trust signals like these can significantly increase your conversion rates and drive more traffic via word-of-mouth referrals.

Content creation for traffic isn't a one-time effort but an ongoing process. Regularly updating your content keeps it relevant and can improve its performance in search rankings. Set aside time each month to review your existing content and update it with the latest trends, data, and insights. This shows search engines and your audience that your site is active and up-to-date.

Incorporate multimedia elements to make your content more engaging. Videos, infographics, and interactive elements can break up text and keep visitors engaged longer. This not only improves the user experience but can also reduce bounce rates, which is good for SEO. Short video clips explaining a complex concept or infographics summarizing key points can cater to different learning styles within your audience.

Collaborations and Partnerships can also amplify your content's reach. Partnering with influencers in your niche can expose your content to a wider audience. Look for influencers whose followers align with your target demographics. Joint ventures such as webinars, podcasts, or co-authored articles can provide value to both audiences, driving traffic and credibility for both parties.

Content distribution is as important as content creation. Share your content across multiple channels including social media, email newsletters, and relevant online communities. Being active in discussions on platforms like Reddit or Quora can also drive traffic back to your site. Don't just drop links; engage in meaningful discussions and provide value to the community. This builds relationships and positions you as an authority figure.

To measure the effectiveness of your content strategy, regularly analyze your traffic data. Tools like Google Analytics can provide insights into which content pieces are driving the most traffic and conversions. Use this data to refine your strategy, doubling down on what works and tweaking or discarding what doesn't. Look at metrics like time on page, bounce rate, and conversion rates to get a comprehensive view of your content's performance.

Remember, content creation for traffic is a marathon, not a sprint. It requires patience, persistence, and a willingness to continually adapt and improve. The digital world is ever-evolving, and so should your content strategy. Stay curious, keep learning, and always focus on providing the best value for your audience. That's how you drive traffic, build a loyal audience, and pave your path to financial freedom.

SEO Basics is your gateway to unlocking the potential of organic traffic, a key component in building a profitable affiliate website that can generate passive income for years to come. Imagine the internet as a vast, bustling city; SEO, or Search Engine Optimization, is your roadmap to navigating this city and setting up shop in the most visible and visited parts of town.

At its core, SEO is a series of strategies and techniques aimed at improving the visibility of your website on search engines like Google. When done correctly, it allows you to attract the right audience without spending a dime on advertising. For those keen on escaping the 9-to-5 grind, mastering SEO basics is akin to finding a goldmine.

Let's break it down. Search engines operate on algorithms that rank websites based on relevance and quality. Your goal with SEO is to ensure your website aligns perfectly with these algorithms. This involves optimizing your site's content, structure, and coding to make it as attractive as possible to search engines.

One of the foundational elements of SEO is keyword research. Keywords are the terms and phrases people enter into search engines when they're looking for information. Identifying high-traffic, low-competition keywords related to your niche can place your content right in front of your target audience. Think of it like setting up a lemonade stand on the busiest street during a hot summer day.

Once you've identified your keywords, it's crucial to incorporate them naturally throughout your website. This includes your site's titles, headings, meta descriptions, and body content. However, avoid the temptation to "stuff" keywords unnaturally; search engines are sophisticated enough to penalize such tactics. Aim to balance between relevancy and readability.

Another vital component is on-page SEO, which involves optimizing individual pages on your site. This starts with creating high-quality, original content that provides real value to your visitors. Your content should be informative, engaging, and tailored to your audience's needs. The more valuable your content, the more likely visitors are to stay on your site, reducing your bounce rate and improving your search engine ranking.

Structured data, or schema markup, is another powerful tool in your SEO arsenal. This is code you add to your website to help search engines understand the content better. It can enhance your search engine listings with additional information like ratings, reviews, and more, making them more appealing to users.

Don't overlook the importance of technical SEO. This involves optimizing the backend structure of your website. Factors such as fast load times, mobile-friendliness, and secure sockets layer (SSL) certificates contribute to a better user experience and higher search engine rankings. A well-structured site is like a well-organized store; visitors can find what they need quickly, leading to higher satisfaction and conversion rates.

Building high-quality backlinks is another critical aspect of SEO. Backlinks are links from other websites that point to your site. Search engines view these as votes of confidence; the more reputable sites link to you, the more authoritative and trustworthy your site appears. You can earn backlinks by creating valuable content others want to share and by building relationships with influencers in your niche.

Social signals are also playing an increasingly important role in SEO. These are the likes, shares, and comments your content receives on social media platforms. While not a direct ranking factor, social signals can drive traffic and generate backlinks, indirectly boosting your SEO efforts. Engage with your audience on social media to amplify your reach and drive more organic traffic to your site.

It's also worth noting that SEO isn't a one-time effort. Search algorithms are constantly evolving, and your competitors are always vying for those top spots. Consistent monitoring and updating of your SEO strategies are vital. Tools like Google Analytics and Google Search Console can provide valuable insights into your site's performance and areas for improvement.

Now, let's talk about local SEO, a must if your affiliate marketing efforts have a local or regional focus. This involves optimizing your site so that it appears in local search results. Claim your business on Google My Business, ensure your name, address, and phone number (NAP) are consistent across all online listings, and gather positive customer reviews to boost your local search rankings.

The ultimate aim of SEO is to build a website that attracts sustained, high-quality traffic. By focusing on what users need and delivering it in the best possible way, you're laying a robust foundation for long-term passive income. Indeed, mastering SEO basics can become one of your most valuable skills in your journey toward financial freedom.

Remember, SEO is not just about getting visitors to your site; it's about attracting the right visitors — those who are likely to engage with your content, click on your affiliate links, and ultimately convert into customers. This targeted approach ensures your efforts yield the highest possible returns.

To wrap up, SEO basics might seem daunting at first, but with consistent effort, the potential rewards make it all worthwhile. Embrace the process, stay updated with changing trends, and keep refining your strategies. Your dedication to understanding and applying SEO fundamentals will pay dividends, turning your affiliate website into a powerful, revenue-generating asset.

Chapter 8:
Dropshipping and E-commerce

Dropshipping and e-commerce offer a fast track to passive income by leveraging the power of the internet to reach a global audience. Setting up an online store has never been easier thanks to platforms like Shopify and WooCommerce, which streamline the process from inventory management to sales analytics. Finding reliable suppliers might seem daunting at first, but numerous resources like AliExpress, Oberlo, and SaleHoo simplify the process, ensuring you get quality products at competitive prices. One of the major advantages of dropshipping is the ability to automate order fulfillment; apps and plugins can handle everything from inventory updates to shipping notifications, allowing you to focus on scaling your business through marketing and customer engagement. The initial setup requires careful planning and a bit of effort, but once in place, a well-run dropshipping store can generate consistent revenue with minimal ongoing effort. Ultimately, this chapter aims to equip you with the knowledge and tools to build a successful e-commerce venture, setting you on a course toward financial freedom through passive income.

Setting Up Your Online Store

Creating an online store is your first critical step in the dropshipping and e-commerce journey. Your store will be the hub where transactions occur, products are showcased, and customer interactions take place. The goal is to build a digital storefront that is not only visually appealing but also functional, easy to navigate, and designed for conversions. Let's walk through the essential steps you'll need to set up an online store that sets you on the path to financial freedom.

First things first, you need to choose the right e-commerce platform for your store. With dozens of options available, it can be overwhelming to pick the best one. Popular platforms like Shopify, WooCommerce, and BigCommerce offer varying features that cater to different levels of expertise and business needs. Look for a platform that provides easy integration with dropshipping suppliers, has customizable templates, and offers excellent customer support.

Once you've selected your platform, it's time to purchase your domain name. Think of your domain name as your store's address on the internet. Aim for something short, memorable, and related to your niche. The right domain name can have a powerful impact on your brand recognition and SEO performance.

Next, you'll need to choose a theme for your online store. Most e-commerce platforms come with a variety of free and paid themes. While it's tempting to go with a free theme, investing in a premium theme can make your store look more professional and offer better customization options. Remember, first impressions matter. A clean, well-designed store can significantly increase your chances of converting visitors into buyers.

After selecting a theme, you'll want to customize it to fit your brand's aesthetic. This entails uploading your logo, choosing a color scheme, and setting up your store's navigation. Your logo should be distinctive and reflect what your store is about. Having a consistent color scheme harmonizes your storefront, making it more visually cohesive and pleasing.

Now, let's talk about product listings. This is where you'll spend a good amount of time, as each product needs detailed descriptions, high-quality images, and accurate pricing. Dropshipping platforms like Oberlo, Spocket, and AliExpress make it easy to import products directly to your store, but don't just use the default descriptions provided by suppliers. Write compelling product descriptions that highlight the benefits and features of each item. High-quality images are also crucial; they allow potential buyers to see exactly what they're purchasing.

A critical aspect of setting up your online store is implementing effective SEO (Search Engine Optimization) strategies. This includes using relevant keywords in your product descriptions, meta tags, and alt texts for images. SEO can significantly impact your store's visibility on search engines, driving organic traffic to your site without the need for paid advertising.

Another important facet is setting up payment gateways. Your customers need multiple ways to pay for their purchases, including credit cards, PayPal, and other digital wallets. Look for a secure, encrypted payment gateway that offers these options while keeping transaction fees low. A seamless checkout process minimizes cart abandonment and maximizes your revenue.

Don't forget to set up your store policies, including shipping, returns, and privacy policies. These policies set clear expectations with your customers and build trust. Transparency in how you handle shipping times, return processes, and data privacy can make or break customer loyalty.

Customer service is paramount in maintaining a successful online store. Implement live chat features, build a comprehensive FAQ section, and consider offering email or phone support. Excellent customer service can turn first-time buyers into repeat customers and even brand advocates.

Once all these foundational elements are in place, it's time to conduct a thorough test of your store before going live. Ensure all buttons, links, and forms work correctly. Place a few test orders to make sure the checkout process is smooth and error-free. A glitchy site can damage your credibility and hurt sales.

Marketing your online store effectively is the final major step to setting it up for success. Utilize social media platforms, email marketing, and pay-per-click (PPC) advertising to drive traffic to your store. Influencer partnerships and collaborations can also provide a significant boost to your brand visibility.

Lastly, be prepared to continually optimize your store. This journey doesn't end once your store is launched; it's an ongoing process. Use analytics tools to track your store's performance and customer behavior. Make adjustments based on this data to enhance user experience and increase conversions.

Setting up your online store is more than just a technical task—it's laying the groundwork for your financial future. By putting in the time, effort, and attention to detail now, you're setting yourself up for long-term success. Stay focused, adaptable, and committed to delivering value to your customers, and you'll be well on your way to escaping the 9-to-5 grind and achieving financial freedom.

Finding Reliable Suppliers

When it comes to dropshipping and e-commerce, the cornerstone of your success lies in finding reliable suppliers. It's not just about sourcing products; your suppliers can make or break your business. Think of them as the backbone of your e-commerce enterprise. Without strong, dependable partners, even the most outstanding storefront will falter. This section dives deep into the strategies and practices for securing trustworthy suppliers who will support your path to financial independence.

The first rule of thumb when looking for suppliers is to do your due diligence. This means thorough research. Don't be swayed by flashy websites or too-good-to-be-true promises. Instead, spend time vetting suppliers. Use platforms like Alibaba, AliExpress, and SaleHoo, but don't rely solely on these sources. You need to dig deeper to ensure you're partnering with credible and reliable suppliers. Check their business licenses, look for third-party certifications, and read as many reviews as you can find.

Another key factor is to establish direct communication with potential suppliers. Don't limit your interactions to emails or messages alone. Whenever possible, get on a call with them. This allows you to ask pointed questions and gauge their responsiveness and professionalism. How quickly do they answer your inquiries? Are they open and transparent about their processes? These interactions can give you a good feel for who you're dealing with.

Quality control should be one of your top priorities. You can't afford to compromise on this. Many suppliers will offer sample products for a nominal fee. Take advantage of this opportunity to examine the quality firsthand. Look for consistency in product specifications, durability, and overall appearance. If the samples don't meet your standards, don't hesitate to move on. In the world of dropshipping, consistent product quality translates to customer satisfaction and repeat business.

Reliability isn't just about the products themselves. A reliable supplier also means consistent lead times and predictable shipping durations. You don't want your customers to wait endlessly for their orders. Discuss shipping terms openly and set clear expectations. Reliable suppliers will have dependable logistics and will be clear about processing and shipping times. Always have a backup supplier lined up to ensure that any disruption in the supply chain doesn't impact your business negatively.

Don't underestimate the power of negotiation. Many new dropshippers feel that the price quoted by the supplier is set in stone. However, many suppliers are open to negotiating prices, especially if you plan to order in bulk. Building a relationship with your suppliers can often lead to better pricing, favorable terms, and even exclusive deals. Ask if there are discounts for high-volume orders or if payment terms can be adjusted to fit your cash flow needs.

Furthermore, use technology to your advantage. Several online tools and platforms help you manage supplier relationships efficiently. Software like Oberlo, Dropified, and Inventory Source integrate seamlessly with e-commerce platforms like Shopify. These tools not only streamline product sourcing but also automate order fulfillment, making your dropshipping business more efficient and less prone to human error.

Your supplier relationship should feel like a partnership. You're not just their customer; you're their business ally. Ensure you maintain open lines of communication and keep your suppliers informed about any changes in order quantities or potential surges in demand. A great supplier will not just fulfill your orders; they'll help you scale by offering insights and even suggesting trending products.

Look out for red flags that signal an unreliable supplier. Unresponsiveness, vague answers, inconsistent product quality, and unclear payment terms can all be warning signs. If a supplier isn't willing to provide samples or dodges your questions, consider it a big red flag. Trust your instincts and don't settle for a supplier that doesn't meet your criteria.

Attending trade shows and industry events can also be an invaluable way to find reliable suppliers. These events offer the opportunity to meet suppliers in person, see their product range, and establish relationships. The personal connections you build can be incredibly beneficial, providing you direct access to the lifeline of your e-commerce business.

It's also important to continuously review supplier performance. Make it a habit to revisit your agreements and assess whether your suppliers are living up to their promises. Are they maintaining quality standards? Are they meeting shipping deadlines? Regular evaluations can help you decide whether to continue the relationship or start looking for better options.

Don't forget about the legal aspects. A solid contract with your suppliers can save you a lot of hassle down the line. Ensure that your contract covers all the critical areas—product quality, shipping terms, payment conditions, and dispute resolution. Having a legally binding agreement makes your supplier relationship more formal, ensuring both parties are clear on their obligations.

By now, it should be clear that finding reliable suppliers is not a task to be taken lightly. It involves meticulous research, honest communication, and often, a bit of trial and error. However, the effort you put in to find dependable suppliers will pay off immensely in the long run. You'll be securing the foundation upon which your entire dropshipping business rests.

Remember, the journey to financial freedom through e-commerce is not just about setting up a store. It's about creating a sustainable and efficient system that can operate with minimal hiccups. By ensuring that you have reliable suppliers, you're one step closer to building a robust passive income stream that will support your goals for years to come.

Automating Order Fulfillment

When you're diving into the world of dropshipping and e-commerce, one of the most transformative elements you can incorporate into your business model is automating order fulfillment. This is the secret sauce that can take you from a part-time gig to a scalable business that runs itself. Let's break down the complexities and show you how mastering this process can be a game-changer for achieving financial freedom.

First things first, what exactly is order fulfillment? Simply put, it's the entire process that happens from the moment a customer places an order to the point they receive their product. This includes inventory management, picking and packing items, shipping, and tracking. When you automate this process, you essentially put your business on autopilot, freeing up your time to focus on other income-generating activities or even enjoy more personal freedom. Essentially, you're building a machine that works for you.

Automation in order fulfillment isn't just about saving time; it's about increasing accuracy and reliability. Think about it: human errors in manually processing orders can lead to unhappy customers and costly mistakes. Automation solves this issue by ensuring every step of the fulfillment process adheres to a standardized, repeatable procedure. This robustness enhances your customer experience, builds your brand reputation, and encourages repeat business.

The technology for automating order fulfillment has never been more accessible. Various software applications and services can integrate seamlessly with your e-commerce platform. For instance, apps like Oberlo (for Shopify) can automatically process orders as soon as they're made. They communicate directly with suppliers, update your inventory in real-time, and even handle shipping and tracking information.

Moreover, many third-party logistics providers (3PLs) offer end-to-end solutions that can handle all aspects of order fulfillment on your behalf. Companies like ShipBob and Fulfillment by Amazon (FBA) are experts in logistics and can manage your stock, packaging, shipping, and returns. By leveraging these services, you can scale your e-commerce business without worrying about the logistical hurdles that come with growth.

Another critical aspect of automating order fulfillment is integrating it with customer relationship management (CRM) systems. When your CRM communicates effectively with your order fulfillment system, you're also automating customer interactions. Automated emails to notify customers of order confirmations, shipping updates, and delivery statuses not only save you time but also keep your customers informed and engaged.

Let's touch on the importance of analytics and feedback loops in this automated ecosystem. An automated order fulfillment system will often come with built-in analytics tools. These tools can offer valuable insights into your supply chain performance, customer satisfaction, and even potential bottlenecks. By analyzing this data, you can continuously optimize your processes, tweak your inventory levels, and refine your shipping strategies to maintain peak efficiency.

Integrating AI and machine learning into your fulfillment process can also add another layer of sophistication. AI algorithms can predict demand patterns, optimize stock levels, and even automate reordering from suppliers. This predictive capability ensures you're always stocked with what's most likely to sell, thereby reducing the risk of stockouts or overstock situations which could tie up your cash flow unnecessarily.

Let's not forget about returns management. Automating this often-overlooked part of the process can significantly improve customer satisfaction. Solutions like Returnly or Happy Returns integrate with your e-commerce platform to provide a seamless returns experience for your customers while ensuring that returned stock is efficiently processed and restocked.

The real beauty of automated order fulfillment lies in its scalability. As your business grows, the same automated processes that handle ten orders a day can handle thousands, all without requiring proportional increases in manpower or overhead. This scalability allows you to focus on other crucial aspects of your business, such as marketing, customer service, and expansion into new markets.

Furthermore, having an automated fulfillment process makes your business attractive to potential investors or buyers. Prospective investors are more likely to consider a business that runs efficiently and with predictable scalability and profitability. It proves that you've established a solid operational foundation capable of supporting sustained growth.

While the benefits are immense, setting up an automated order fulfillment system requires an initial investment of time and resources. You'll need to choose the right software and 3PL partners, integrate these platforms seamlessly, and test the system rigorously to iron out any kinks. But trust me, the upfront investment is worth the long-term gains.

You're not just setting up a business; you're creating a lifestyle that isn't shackled to daily operational tasks. Automation empowers you to manage multiple streams of passive income efficiently and effectively, all while gaining more freedom to invest your time where it matters most—whether that's in growing your business further, exploring new ventures, or simply enjoying life with your family and friends.

In conclusion, automating order fulfillment is one of the most impactful steps you can take in your dropshipping and e-commerce journey. It's a cornerstone strategy for building a scalable, robust, and hassle-free business that aligns perfectly with the ultimate goal of achieving financial freedom. As you take this critical step, you'll find yourself well on your way to creating a sustainable, passive income stream that supports your long-term financial independence.

Chapter 9:
Blogging as a Business

Creating a blog isn't just a hobby—it's a potential goldmine when approached with the right mindset and strategy. Imagine tapping into your passions and transforming them into a profitable venture that earns while you sleep. The key is to start with a well-defined niche and a robust content strategy that attracts and engages your target audience. Once your blog gains traction, monetizing becomes a multi-faceted endeavor with opportunities ranging from advertising revenue to sponsored content. Each blog post you publish is a building block towards financial freedom, allowing for scalability and diversification. To thrive, focus on authentic connection and delivering real value through your content, making your blog an indispensable resource for readers. This journey demands patience and persistence, but the rewards—both financial and personal—are well worth the effort. So, step into the world of blogging with a business mindset, and watch as your words pave the way to a life of independence and financial security.

niche selection and content strategy

Selecting the right niche could be the difference between a thriving blog and one that struggles to gain traction. When it comes to blogging as a business, niche selection isn't just about choosing a topic you like; it's about finding a subject that you're passionate about and that also has a viable market. You want a niche that you're knowledgeable about but also one that has enough audience interest to generate sustainable traffic and income.

First, let's talk about passion. Passion will fuel your persistence and keep you motivated even when the going gets tough. Remember, you're creating a business here, and just like any other business, there'll be ups and downs. Passion will help you ride through those waves. But, passion alone isn't enough. You need to validate that your chosen niche has market potential. This involves some market research to see if there's demand for the content you plan to offer.

A good starting point is to identify broad topics that interest you, then drill down into more specific sub-niches. For example, if you're interested in fitness, you could narrow it down to niche topics like keto diets, home workouts, or mental health and wellness. These sub-niches can often have less competition and more targeted audiences, making it easier for you to gain traction quickly compared to going after a broader market.

Market research tools can be extremely beneficial at this stage. Platforms like Google Trends, SEMrush, and Ahrefs can help you assess the competitiveness and demand for various niches. Look for niches with steady or growing search interest but not overwhelmingly high competition. The sweet spot is a niche with moderate competition and a die-hard audience willing to spend money on products or services related to it.

Next, let's consider your unique value proposition (UVP). What makes your blog stand out from the crowded blogosphere? Your UVP is what differentiates you from others operating in the same niche. This could be your unique background, experience, writing style, or even a fresh perspective on a familiar topic. The more distinct and appealing your UVP, the more likely you are to attract and retain a loyal audience.

Determining your content strategy goes hand in hand with selecting your niche. You'll need to decide on the types of content you'll produce. Will it be how-to articles, personal stories, interviews, product reviews, or a combination of these? Knowing your audience and understanding what type of content resonates most with them will be critical for this step. Tailor your content to solve specific problems or answer questions your target audience has.

Content creation should be driven by an understanding of your audience's needs and behaviors. Understand their pain points, what keeps them awake at night, and create content that provides real solutions. Engaging content isn't just about good writing; it's about relevance and utility. Each piece of content should serve a specific purpose, whether it's educational, inspirational, or entertaining.

In addition to written content, consider diversifying the types of content you produce. Videos, podcasts, infographics, and social media posts can help you reach different segments of your audience. A multifaceted content strategy not only keeps your audience engaged but also opens up multiple avenues for monetization.

SEO (Search Engine Optimization) should not be overlooked. While it's a vast topic on its own, the basics of SEO can make a massive difference in your blog's visibility. Use keyword research to identify high-value keywords in your niche and incorporate them naturally into your content. Meta descriptions, alt tags for images, and internal linking are all SEO practices that can boost your blog's search engine ranking.

Creating a content calendar is a strategic move to ensure consistency. Consistency builds trust and keeps your audience coming back for more. A content calendar organizes your posting schedule and helps you plan content around key dates, industry events, or trending topics in your niche. Use tools like Trello or Asana to map out your content plan and stick to it.

Social media can turbocharge your content strategy. Promoting your blog content on platforms like Facebook, Instagram, and Twitter can drive significant traffic to your blog. Each platform has its unique strengths, so tailor your content and promotion strategy accordingly. Social media can also provide instant feedback from your audience, allowing you to tweak your strategy in real-time.

Networking with other bloggers in your niche can be incredibly beneficial. Guest blogging, collaborative posts, or even simple shout-outs can give you access to a broader audience. Networking also opens doors to learning opportunities, where experienced bloggers can provide valuable insights and advice.

Let's not forget email marketing. Building an email list from day one enables you to have direct access to your audience. Offering lead magnets like eBooks, checklists, or exclusive content in exchange for email sign-ups can be an effective way to grow your list. Use email marketing campaigns to nurture your audience, keep them engaged, and direct traffic back to your blog.

Analyzing performance metrics will help you refine your content strategy. Tools like Google Analytics can offer insights into which posts are performing well, how users are interacting with your content, and where your traffic is coming from. Use these insights to produce more of what works and less of what doesn't.

In conclusion, your niche selection and content strategy are foundational elements of your blogging business. They require careful planning, consistent effort, and ongoing adjustments. By choosing a niche that aligns with your passion and market demand, and developing a robust content strategy, you set the stage for a successful and profitable blog. Commitment, adaptability, and relentless focus on delivering value to your audience will pave the way for your blogging success.

Monetizing Your Blog

When it comes to monetizing your blog, the options at your disposal are vast, yet each requires a strategic approach to unlock its full potential. Whether you're aiming to earn through advertising revenue or landing lucrative sponsored content deals, the key is to create high-quality, engaging content that attracts and retains a dedicated audience. Ads can be seamlessly integrated through platforms like Google AdSense, bringing in income with every click, while sponsored posts allow you to collaborate with brands that resonate with your readers. Diversify your monetization strategies by incorporating affiliate marketing links within your posts, offering value to your audience through product recommendations that earn you a commission. Remember, the goal here is to establish multiple streams of income from your blog, turning it into a sustainable, passive revenue generator. By continuously providing valuable content and building trust with your audience, you'll set the stage for long-term profitability and financial independence.

Advertising Revenue has been the backbone for many successful bloggers, turning their platforms into profitable ventures. At its core, advertising revenue is the money earned by allowing companies to display ads on your blog. Whether you're leveraging banner ads, sponsored posts, or more sophisticated ad networks, the potential for income is vast if managed correctly.

The first key point to understand is the diverse range of advertising options available to you. One of the most straightforward methods involves display ads, which can be set up through ad networks like Google AdSense. These networks pay you based on the number of visitors who see or interact with the ads on your blog. Imagine each visitor as a potential dollar sign; the more traffic you drive to your site, the higher your potential revenue.

Another lucrative option is through sponsored content. This involves writing posts or creating content tailored to the needs of a sponsor. Companies pay handsomely for personalized content that aligns with their brand, especially if your blog has a substantial and engaged following. This method requires a bit more effort and negotiation but can result in significant earnings.

For those looking to diversify further, affiliate marketing can complement your traditional ad revenue streams. By promoting products or services relevant to your audience and earning a commission from each sale made through your referral, you can double-dip on income without overwhelming your blog with ads. We'll dive deeper into affiliate marketing in another chapter, but keep in mind its synergy with advertising revenue.

It's important to talk about the scalability of advertising revenue. One of the most attractive aspects of this income stream is its scalability. Initially, you might only earn a small amount, but as your blog grows, so does your earning potential. This scalability is particularly empowering because it means that with consistent effort and strategic planning, you can exponentially increase your income over time.

To optimize your advertising revenue, it's crucial to understand your audience. Knowing what interests them, what type of content they engage with the most, and how they interact with your blog will help you tailor your advertising strategy. Tools like Google Analytics can provide insights into visitor demographics and behavior, allowing you to make data-driven decisions that maximize your income.

Next, consider the user experience. Too many advertisements can dilute the quality of your blog and drive away your audience. There's a delicate balance between monetization and maintaining an enjoyable user experience. Ideally, ads should be relevant and unobtrusive, integrated seamlessly within your content so they don't feel forced or overwhelming.

A/B testing is another strategy to help optimize your advertising placements. By experimenting with different ad layouts, formats, and positions on your blog, you can determine which combination yields the highest return. Continuous tweaking and testing will help you find the sweet spot that maximizes revenue without sacrificing user satisfaction.

Ad blockers are a growing concern for bloggers relying on advertising revenue. As more internet users employ ad blockers to enhance their browsing experience, fewer ads are shown, which translates to lower revenue. One way to combat this is by creating exceptional, high-quality content that encourages users to whitelist your blog. Building a loyal community that values your content can also support alternative revenue models like subscription services or merchandise sales.

Moreover, don't disregard the importance of SEO (Search Engine Optimization). By optimizing your content for search engines, you can attract more organic traffic to your blog, which in turn increases ad impressions and clicks. Higher traffic directly correlates with higher advertising revenue, so investing time in learning and implementing SEO best practices can pay huge dividends.

Understand that blogging as a business involves continual learning and adaptation. The digital landscape is ever-evolving, with new ad platforms, technologies, and strategies emerging regularly. Staying updated with the latest trends and continuously refining your approach will help you stay ahead in the game and keep your advertising revenue stream robust.

Networking with other bloggers and joining blogging communities can also provide valuable insights and opportunities for cross-promotion. Sharing experiences and strategies with peers can open up new ideas and potentially fruitful collaborations, further boosting your blog's reach and advertising revenue.

Transparency is another key aspect when it comes to sponsored content and ads. Maintaining trust with your audience by being open about paid promotions can build long-term loyalty and respect. People appreciate honesty and are more likely to support your monetization efforts if they feel you're being genuine.

Finally, remember that patience and persistence are paramount. Building a blog that generates substantial advertising revenue doesn't happen overnight. It requires consistent effort, strategic planning, and an unwavering commitment to producing quality content. Your blog is a long-term investment, one that can indeed yield significant passive income with the right balance of time, effort, and strategy.

In essence, monetizing your blog through advertising is a multifaceted endeavor. By understanding your audience, optimizing user experience, leveraging SEO, and continually learning and adapting, you can create a steady stream of income that grows with your blog's popularity. Use this knowledge as a stepping stone on your journey toward financial freedom and independence.

Sponsored Content can be a powerful tool in your passive income arsenal and one that offers immense potential for monetizing your blog. Sponsored content, simply put, involves creating and publishing content paid for by a brand or a company looking to promote its products or services. Unlike traditional advertising, sponsored content integrates naturally with your blog's material, providing valuable information to your readers while subtly promoting the sponsor's offering.

To get started with sponsored content, the first critical step is ensuring your blog has a well-defined niche and consistent traffic.

Brands are more likely to sponsor content on blogs that attract a specific audience and show steady growth in reader engagement. If your blog covers broad topics, narrowing down to a more targeted audience can offer a clearer value proposition to potential sponsors. For example, a blog focused strictly on eco-friendly living is more appealing to brands in the green industry than a general lifestyle blog.

When approaching potential sponsors, it's crucial to have a media kit ready. This kit should include your blog's analytics, audience demographics, and social media reach. Additionally, showcase examples of past successful collaborations if you have any. This demonstrates your capacity to create engaging sponsored content that resonates with your audience and meets the sponsor's goals.

Transparency and authenticity are paramount in sponsored content. Your audience trusts you for honest recommendations and insights, and that trust is the foundation of your blog's success. Clearly disclose sponsored posts to maintain credibility. Use straightforward language like "This post is sponsored by [Brand]" or "In partnership with [Brand]" at the beginning of the content. This ensures readers know upfront about the sponsorship, respecting their right to transparency.

Crafting effective sponsored content requires a balance between promotional material and genuine value. Instead of presenting an overt advertisement, focus on how the sponsor's product or service solves a real problem for your audience. For instance, if you run a fitness blog, a sponsored post might detail how a particular brand's workout gear enhances performance or comfort, backed by your personal experience or testimonials from your readers.

Consistency in tone and style is another critical element. Sponsored posts should seamlessly blend with your regular content, maintaining the same voice and format your readers are accustomed to.

This not only preserves the reader's experience but also enhances the sponsor's message by delivering it in a trusted, familiar context.

Performance tracking is essential for long-term success in sponsored content. Utilize analytics tools to monitor how sponsored posts perform in terms of traffic, engagement, and conversions. Share these insights with your sponsors to demonstrate value and build long-term partnerships. Effective reporting can also help you negotiate better rates and secure more collaborations in the future.

Pricing your sponsored content fairly can be challenging, particularly when you're just starting out. Consider factors like your blog's traffic, audience engagement, and the time required to create the content. You can set rates per post, offer package deals, or even propose long-term partnerships for recurring collaborations. Starting with competitive, fair pricing will build your reputation and encourage repeat business from satisfied sponsors.

Building relationships with brands involves more than just closing sponsorship deals. Engage with companies within your niche by liking, sharing, and commenting on their social media posts. Attend industry events or webinars where you might network with brand representatives. Personal connections often lead to lucrative sponsorship deals and strengthen professional ties within your industry.

Sponsored content must also align with your personal brand and values. Not all sponsorships will be a good fit, and turning down offers that don't align with your blog's ethos is sometimes necessary. For example, if your blog promotes vegan living, a sponsorship from a meat product company would conflict with your content and alienate your audience. Staying true to your principles ensures long-term trust and loyalty from your readers.

Leveraging multiple channels can amplify the effectiveness of your sponsored content. Cross-promote your sponsored posts on social media, email newsletters, and even through guest posts on related blogs. The more visibility your sponsored content gains, the more value you provide to your sponsor, enhancing the likelihood of future collaborations.

Creating high-quality visuals and multimedia can further engage your audience with sponsored content. Eye-catching images, informative videos, and interactive elements can distinguish your sponsored posts from standard text-based content. Invest in good design tools or hire freelance designers and videographers if necessary, as compelling visuals significantly boost reader engagement.

Feedback from both your audience and sponsors is invaluable in refining your sponsored content strategy. Encourage reader feedback through comments and surveys, and regularly ask sponsors for their satisfaction and improvements. This two-way communication fosters better-sponsored posts that meet everyone's needs and enhances your credibility as a reliable partner.

Lastly, maintain ethical standards throughout your sponsored content endeavors. Adhering to FTC guidelines on disclosures and following best practices in content creation upholds the trust you've built with your audience. Ethical sponsorship practices not only protect you from legal complications but also solidify your reputation as a trustworthy and professional blogger.

In conclusion, sponsored content offers a viable and profitable method for monetizing your blog while providing valuable information to your readers. By approaching it with authenticity, transparency, and a focus on delivering value, you can build strong partnerships with brands and create a sustainable income stream. Remember, the key to successful sponsored content lies in maintaining the balance between promotional content and the genuine value your audience seeks.

Chapter 10:
Leveraging Social Media Platforms

In today's digital age, your path to financial freedom could be just a few clicks away, thanks to social media platforms. With billions of active users across YouTube, Instagram, and podcasting platforms, leveraging these powerful tools can transform your passive income streams into a robust and sustainable source of wealth. Whether it's creating engaging video content on YouTube to earn ad revenue and sponsorships or utilizing Instagram to build a brand and foster influencer marketing deals, the possibilities are endless. Podcasting is another thriving avenue that allows you to reach a niche audience and generate income through sponsorships and affiliate marketing. Each of these platforms comes with its own set of strategies and best practices, but the core principle remains the same: consistently provide value, engage with your audience, and monetize through various streams. By strategically utilizing social media, you can expand your reach, create diverse income channels, and ultimately secure your financial independence.

Youtube Revenue Streams

When it comes to generating passive income through social media, YouTube stands out as one of the most lucrative platforms. Whether you're passionate about creating engaging content or looking for a way to monetize your existing talents, building a YouTube channel can be a game-changer in your quest for financial freedom. But YouTube revenue doesn't come from just one source. It's a multifaceted platform offering multiple streams of income.

First on the list is AdSense revenue, the bread and butter for many YouTubers. Once you've reached the threshold of 1,000 subscribers and 4,000 watch hours, you can join the YouTube Partner Program. This program allows you to earn money from ads that play before, during, or after your videos. Though the income can vary depending on factors like niche, viewer demographics, and engagement, it's a significant starting point for passive income.

Another compelling revenue stream is affiliate marketing. This involves promoting products or services within your videos or descriptions. When viewers click on your affiliate links and make purchases, you earn a commission. Channels that offer reviews, tutorials, or lifestyle content often find this method particularly effective. The key is to promote products you genuinely believe in, as authenticity drives higher conversions.

Sponsorship deals offer another lucrative avenue. Brands are constantly on the lookout for influencers with engaged audiences. Once your channel gains traction, you can collaborate with brands willing to pay for dedicated videos, shout-outs, or product placements. These deals can be exceptionally profitable, particularly for channels in niches like tech, beauty, and fitness. It's vital to negotiate terms that align with your brand values and audience expectations.

Merchandise sales should not be overlooked. You can create and sell your own branded products, such as t-shirts, mugs, or digital downloads. YouTube even facilitates this through its Merch Shelf feature, which allows eligible channels to display their products directly below their videos. Leveraging your unique brand to create merch can add a personalized touch to your revenue streams.

Memberships and subscriptions present additional opportunities for recurring income. YouTube offers a channel memberships feature where viewers can pay a monthly fee for exclusive perks like behind-the-scenes content, member-only live streams, or early access to new videos. Patreon is another platform that complements YouTube by enabling fans to support their favorite creators through monthly contributions in exchange for exclusive content and rewards.

Super Chats and Super Stickers engage your audience during live streams while adding to your income. Viewers can purchase these interactive features to highlight their messages or show appreciation during live broadcasts. It's a brilliant way to monetize live interactions and build a deeper connection with your audience.

Creating and selling online courses or workshops can also be a natural extension of a successful YouTube channel. If you possess expertise or skills that your audience wants to learn, packaging this knowledge into paid courses can create another substantial revenue stream. Promote these courses through your videos, driving organic interest and enrollments.

Consulting and coaching opportunities often arise for channels that establish authority in their niche. Whether you offer one-on-one sessions, group webinars, or consultative services, these engagements can command premium fees. They also provide an intimate way to connect with your audience while adding to your income pile.

It's essential to consider the long-term potential of YouTube revenue streams. Applying SEO strategies to your video titles, descriptions, and tags can enhance discoverability and boost your channel's growth. Consistently creating high-quality, valuable content helps you build a loyal audience, laying the groundwork for sustainable passive income.

Another consideration is content repurposing. By transforming your YouTube videos into blog posts, podcasts, or social media snippets, you can extend your reach and potentially tap into additional revenue avenues. Cross-promoting your content across multiple platforms maximizes your content's lifecycle and income potential.

Think about collaborations, too. Partnering with other YouTubers in your niche can introduce your channel to new audiences, driving subscriber growth and engagement. These collaborations don't just expand your reach; they often create a multiplying effect on your earnings through shared subscribers and increased views.

While the start might be slow and earnings might appear negligible at first, the compound effect of multiple revenue streams can be profound. Building a successful YouTube channel requires dedication and consistency, much like any other passive income endeavor. The goal is to set up a system that eventually works for you, even when you're not actively producing new content.

Ultimately, YouTube's potential for generating passive income is immense. By diversifying your revenue streams—advertising, affiliate marketing, sponsorships, merchandise, memberships, super chats, online courses, consulting, and collaborations—you create a robust financial foundation. This not only leads to financial independence but also allows you the freedom to focus on what you love doing.

It's time to harness the power of YouTube. With thoughtful strategy, creativity, and persistence, you'll find that the possibilities are endless.

Instagram Influencer Marketing

In today's digital age, social media platforms play a crucial role in shaping the landscape of passive income opportunities. One of the most potent tools at your disposal is Instagram influencer marketing.

Leveraging this platform can significantly boost your passive income streams if executed correctly. Interestingly, Instagram transcends being just a photo-sharing app; it is an arena teeming with potential for generating substantial financial returns.

Let's start with the basics. Becoming an Instagram influencer entails creating a profile that attracts a dedicated following. Your followers should genuinely care about your content and trust your recommendations. This is primarily achieved by consistently posting high-quality content in a specific niche. Whether it's fitness, travel, lifestyle, or cooking, find your lane and stick to it. Consistency is not just key; it's non-negotiable.

One of the primary ways Instagram influencers monetize their following is through sponsored posts. Brands are continuously looking for authentic voices to promote their products. Once you've established a decent following, you can collaborate with brands that align with your niche and values. This ensures your sponsored content feels natural rather than forced, maintaining follower trust while generating income.

Another effective strategy is affiliate marketing. By promoting products through unique affiliate links, you earn a commission on each sale made through your link. This method requires promoting products you believe in and would recommend even if there were no monetary benefit. Transparency is imperative, as your followers will appreciate honesty and authenticity, which helps in building long-term trust.

Instagram's "Swipe Up" feature in Stories is a game-changer for influencers, allowing seamless integration of affiliate links. Once you hit 10,000 followers, you unlock this feature, making it simpler for your audience to purchase items through your referral. This convenience can significantly amplify your passive income without feeling invasive to your followers.

There are also opportunities for creating and selling your products or services directly through Instagram. From launching e-books to offering online courses or even selling merchandise, your options are diverse. By leveraging Instagram Shopping, you can create a storefront directly on your profile, streamlining the sales process for your followers.

Engagement is another crucial element. It's not enough to have a large number of followers; your engagement rate needs to reflect genuine interaction. Respond to comments, engage in direct messages, and participate in discussions related to your niche. This interaction strengthens your relationship with your audience, making them more likely to support your monetization efforts.

Don't overlook the power of Instagram's analytics tools, either. By consistently analyzing metrics like engagement rate, reach, and impressions, you can fine-tune your content strategy to better serve your audience and attract more lucrative sponsorships. Brands are more likely to collaborate with influencers who can demonstrate their effectiveness with hard data.

If you're looking to scale your influence more quickly, consider collaborating with other influencers. Cross-promotion can benefit both parties by exposing each influencer to the other's audience. This tactic can accelerate your growth and attract followers who are genuinely interested in your content, thereby increasing your monetization potential.

One often-overlooked revenue stream is selling exclusive content. Platforms like Patreon allow influencers to offer premium content to their most loyal followers for a subscription fee. This could include behind-the-scenes looks, detailed tutorials, or one-on-one interaction sessions. It's an excellent way to generate recurring income while rewarding your most engaged fans.

Optimizing your Instagram bio is fundamental. It's usually the first thing people see when they visit your profile, so make it impactful. Include a compelling call-to-action and a link to your blog, e-commerce site, or any other platform you wish to promote. Think of your bio as prime real estate; make every character count.

Keep in mind that Instagram is continuously evolving. Stay adaptable and keep an eye out for new features and trends. For instance, Instagram Reels has become a potent tool for reaching a wider audience. By staying updated and incorporating new features into your strategy, you can maintain and grow your influence.

While it may seem like a glamorous lifestyle, being an Instagram influencer does require consistent effort and creativity. However, the rewards can be immense. From brand partnerships to affiliate marketing to selling your own products, the possibilities for generating passive income are vast and varied.

Lastly, it's essential to treat this like a business. Keep track of your earnings, understand the tax implications, and possibly consult a financial advisor. Proper management of your income streams will ensure sustainability and long-term financial security.

In conclusion, Instagram influencer marketing offers a lucrative avenue for those willing to put in the time and effort. By focusing on authentic engagement, leveraging analytics, and diversifying your income streams, you can create a profitable and sustainable source of passive income. So go ahead, harness the power of Instagram, and watch as your financial dreams inch closer to reality.

Podcasting Profitably

Podcasting has rapidly transformed from a niche hobby to a mainstream medium with immense monetization potential. If you're considering diving into this field, you're in for an enlightenment. Let's break down how to turn your passion for podcasting into a lucrative income stream using the power of social media.

First and foremost, content is king. Your podcast needs to resonate with your target audience. Identifying a specific niche or solving a unique problem can differentiate you from the multitude of podcasts available. Maybe your passion is financial literacy for young adults, or you have an encyclopedic knowledge of '90s pop culture—whatever it is, let your authenticity and expertise shine.

Once your content direction is clear, it's time to leverage social media platforms for both growth and profitability. Social media can amplify your podcast's reach, build a loyal community, and, most importantly, open multiple revenue streams.

Start by creating profiles for your podcast on major social media platforms like Instagram, Facebook, Twitter, and LinkedIn. Each platform has its unique user demographic and engagement level, and understanding this can help you tailor your content accordingly. Instagram, for example, is visual-centric, so sharing behind-the-scenes photos, episode teasers, and even meme content related to your podcast theme can drive engagement.

Consistency is crucial. Establish a posting schedule that ensures your audience always has something to look forward to. This could be regular updates, episode releases, or interactive Q&A sessions. Use stories and reels to give quick updates or behind-the-scenes looks, keeping your audience engaged between episodes.

Don't underestimate the power of collaboration. Engaging with other podcasters and influencers in your niche can introduce your podcast to a broader audience. Guest appearances and cross-promotion are excellent ways to grow your listener base. Additionally, inviting a guest with a significant social media following can result in cross-promotion, where your guest shares their episode with their followers, driving traffic to your podcast.

Monetizing your podcast can take several forms. One of the simplest and most effective ways is through sponsorships and advertising. Once you have a steady listener base, you can reach out to brands that align with your podcast's niche. Whether it's financial services for a finance podcast or eco-friendly products for a sustainability podcast, ensure the brands are relevant to your audience to keep the sponsorships organic.

On social media, using sponsored posts is another lucrative avenue. If your podcast account has significant followers, brands may pay you to post about their products or services. Remember to comply with FTC guidelines by clearly marking these posts as sponsored.

Affiliate marketing offers another revenue stream. Join affiliate programs that resonate with your content and promote these products or services to your audience. Use trackable links in your show notes and social media bios to earn commissions on sales generated through your referral.

Consider setting up a Patreon or a similar membership platform. This can provide exclusive content and perks to your most loyal listeners, who are willing to pay for premium access. Offering bonus episodes, early releases, or exclusive Q&A sessions can significantly add to your monthly revenue.

Engage with your audience through social media polls and questions to understand their needs and preferences better. This interaction enhances the listener experience and provides valuable insights into content creation and monetization strategies. Your audience can become a crucial feedback loop, helping you tweak and enhance your offerings.

Don't forget the power of repurposing content. Your podcast episodes can be transcribed into blog posts, articles, and social media snippets. This not only maximizes the reach of your content but also improves SEO, driving more organic traffic to your platforms.

Lastly, track your metrics diligently. Most social media platforms provide analytics tools that can help you understand what's working and what's not. Monitor engagement rates, follower growth, and traffic driven to your podcast. These insights will guide your strategy, ensuring that your efforts align with your goals.

By leveraging social media effectively, your podcast can grow from a modest endeavor to a profitable venture. The key lies in understanding your audience, being consistent, and continuously exploring monetization opportunities. Remember, every big podcast started small, and with the right strategies, yours can skyrocket to success.

The journey of podcasting profitably is as thrilling as it is rewarding. With dedication, creativity, and strategic use of social media platforms, you'll not only find financial freedom but also foster a community of listeners who value your voice. So, go on, start recording, and let the world hear what you have to say!

Chapter 11:
Email Marketing and List Building

Email marketing remains one of the most powerful tools in your passive income arsenal; it's all about connecting directly with your audience and building relationships that convert over time. By strategically offering a lead magnet—a useful resource that your target audience values—you can grow your email list exponentially. Once these contacts are part of your list, crafting effective email campaigns becomes crucial. This means delivering well-timed, relevant, and engaging content that keeps your audience interested and clicking. Imagine automating parts of this process—scheduling emails in advance or using audience segmentation tools, so the right message reaches the right person at the perfect time, without constant manual effort. This creates a system where you can nurture potential customers while you focus on other income-generating activities. It's not just about sending emails; it's about sending the right emails, consistently, and letting your automated systems do the heavy lifting to sustain and grow your passive income streams.

Creating a Lead Magnet

In the world of email marketing and list building, a lead magnet is your golden ticket. Picture it as the irresistible bait that lures a fish—except in this case, the "fish" are potential subscribers, and the "bait" is a valuable piece of content they're willing to exchange their contact information for. Creating an effective lead magnet can significantly boost your email list, serving as a stepping stone toward financial freedom by leveraging your newfound audience for passive income.

The first step in creating a compelling lead magnet is understanding your target audience. Who are they? What problems are they facing? What solutions are they actively seeking out? Without a clear idea of whom you're targeting, your efforts may be akin to shooting arrows in the dark. Take the time to research, engage, and understand your potential subscribers to ensure your lead magnet hits all the right notes.

Once you have a good grasp of your audience, brainstorm content that would be valuable enough for them to trade their email address. Common types of lead magnets include eBooks, checklists, templates, webinars, and exclusive reports. The key here is not to generalize but rather offer something closely aligned with your audience's interests and pain points. It's about offering a clear solution or actionable information that will make their lives easier or help them achieve something significant.

At this point, it's essential to remember that value trumps quantity. You don't need to create a hundred-page eBook if a well-crafted, ten-page checklist or a detailed one-page infographic will do the job. The goal is to deliver high-impact, bite-sized pieces of information that provide immediate benefits and demonstrate your expertise.

Next, focus on the design and presentation. In an era where attention spans are incredibly short, your lead magnet should be visually appealing and easy to digest. Utilize professional tools or hire a designer if necessary. High-quality graphics, a clean layout, and succinct copy make a significant difference in how your lead magnet is perceived. A well-designed lead magnet reflects professionalism and builds trust, laying the groundwork for a long-term relationship with your subscribers.

Don't underestimate the power of a compelling title. The title of your lead magnet should grab attention and promise value. Instead of generic titles like "How to Save Money," go for something more enticing like "10 Proven Strategies to Save $500 a Month Without Sacrificing Joy". An appealing title can significantly boost your download rates by making your lead magnet seem indispensable.

Distribution is another critical element. Make sure your lead magnet is prominently featured on your website, blog posts, social media channels, and anywhere else you have a digital presence. Use strategically placed opt-in forms and landing pages to capture email addresses. Many successful marketers employ pop-ups, slide-ins, and content upgrades to maximize their lead magnet's reach.

Once your lead magnet is ready to go, you must have a well-thought-out follow-up strategy in place. After someone downloads your lead magnet, they should immediately receive an email that thanks them for their interest and sets the stage for future communications. This welcome email should be friendly, non-salesy, and should deliver what was promised immediately. Consider this a warm handshake - the beginning of a new relationship.

Your follow-up strategy shouldn't end there. Plan a series of emails—often referred to as an autoresponder sequence—that continue to deliver value, nurture your new subscriber relationship, and gradually introduce them to your paid offerings. These emails should build on the initial promise of your lead magnet, providing further insights, tips, and relevant content that solidifies your authority in your niche.

Analytics play a crucial role in optimizing the effectiveness of your lead magnet. Keep an eye on key metrics like download rates, open rates, click-through rates, and conversion rates. These figures offer valuable insights into what's working and where adjustments are needed. A/B testing different elements, from titles and designs to the sequence of follow-up emails, can yield significant improvements over time.

Don't be afraid to refine and iterate. What works today may not work tomorrow, and trends change. Continually gather feedback and stay responsive to the evolving needs of your audience. Your ability to adapt and improve will keep you ahead of the curve and ensure that your list-building efforts remain fruitful.

Another often overlooked aspect is compliance with data protection laws. Make sure you have proper consent mechanisms in place and that your data collection and storage practices comply with regulations like GDPR or CAN-SPAM Act. This not only builds trust with your audience but also safeguards you from potential legal issues.

Lastly, remember that the ultimate goal of your lead magnet isn't just to grow your list—it's to cultivate a relationship with your audience that can be leveraged for passive income opportunities. Whether it's through affiliate marketing, digital product sales, or any other monetization strategies, your lead magnet is the first step in converting curiosity into commitment and, eventually, into recurring revenue.

So go ahead, craft that perfect lead magnet. Not only will it accelerate your path to financial freedom, but it will also empower you to build a community of loyal followers who value what you have to offer. When done right, a lead magnet isn't just a list-building tool; it's a gateway to achieving long-term financial security and independence.

Crafting Effective Email Campaigns

In the world of email marketing, a well-crafted email campaign is both an art and a science. It's not just about writing emails; it's about creating a strategy that connects with your audience on a deeper level, drives engagement, and ultimately, converts. Let's dive into what makes an email campaign effective, especially for those aiming to build multiple streams of passive income and achieve financial freedom.

Firstly, personalization is key. Gone are the days when a generic email would suffice. Today's readers crave personalized content that speaks directly to their interests and needs. Utilizing data, whether it's from customer purchase history or their behavior on your website, allows you to tailor your content specifically for them. A personalized email makes your reader feel valued, increasing the likelihood of opening future emails.

Next, understanding the customer journey can significantly enhance your email marketing efforts. Each subscriber is at a different stage in their journey with you, and recognizing this can help you send more relevant emails. For instance, a new subscriber might appreciate a welcome series that introduces your brand and what you offer. In contrast, a long-term subscriber might be more interested in exclusive offers or advanced content.

Speaking of content, your emails need to provide value. This is not the time for hard selling. Think of your email campaigns as a way to build a relationship with your subscribers. Offer them tips, insights, and solutions to their problems. Educational content that aligns with their interests will not only keep them engaged but also position you as an authority in your field.

Another crucial aspect is your subject line. It's the first thing your subscribers see, and it can make or break your open rates. A compelling subject line should be clear, concise, and enticing. Avoid using spammy words, as they can trigger spam filters and decrease your deliverability. Run A/B tests to see what types of subject lines work best with your audience.

Your email's design and layout also play significant roles. A clean, visually appealing layout with a clear call-to-action (CTA) is essential.

Readers should quickly understand the email's purpose and what you want them to do next. Whether it's clicking a link, reading a blog post, or purchasing a product, your CTA should be prominent and compelling.

Segmentation is another layer of sophistication in effective email campaigns. By categorizing your subscribers based on criteria like demographics, purchase behavior, or engagement levels, you can send more targeted campaigns. This approach ensures that your emails are relevant to each segment, which can significantly boost your engagement and conversion rates.

Timing also matters. The best email in the world won't help if it lands in your subscriber's inbox at the wrong time. Analyzing when your audience is most likely to open their emails can inform the optimal send times. Many email marketing platforms offer analytics to help determine these peak times.

Automation is a game-changer for scaling your email marketing efforts. Automated workflows can nurture leads without you having to lift a finger. Whether it's a welcome series for new subscribers or re-engagement campaigns for inactive users, automation ensures that the right message reaches the right person at the right time. This, in turn, keeps your audience engaged while freeing up your time for other tasks.

It's also worth focusing on the quality of your email list. A smaller, highly engaged list often outperforms a larger, less engaged one. Continually clean your list by removing inactive subscribers who haven't opened your emails over a certain period. This practice maintains your list's health, improves deliverability, and ensures your emails land in the inboxes of those who want to hear from you.

Measuring the success of your campaigns is crucial. Key metrics like open rates, click-through rates, conversion rates, and ROI provide insights into what's working and what needs adjustment. Use this data to refine your strategies continually. Split testing different elements, from subject lines to email copy and design, can offer valuable insights that drive better results over time.

Finally, always respect your subscribers' preferences and privacy. Make it easy for them to unsubscribe, and never buy email lists. Building your list organically might take longer, but it's worth it because those subscribers are genuinely interested in what you offer. Being transparent and ethical builds trust and fosters long-term relationships with your audience.

At the end of the day, an effective email campaign is about more than just marketing your products or services—it's about building a community. When subscribers feel like they're part of something bigger, they're more likely to stay engaged and, ultimately, convert into loyal customers, helping you achieve that financial freedom through multiple streams of passive income.

In summary, mastering the art of email campaigns involves a mix of personalization, understanding your audience's journey, providing valuable content, and leveraging smart design and segmentation. Combined with the power of automation and ongoing analysis, you can create impactful campaigns that resonate with your audience and drive significant results.

Remember, it's a continuous process of learning and adapting. The landscape of email marketing is ever-evolving, and staying agile and receptive to new trends and technologies will keep you at the forefront of your subscribers' inboxes. By implementing these strategies, you'll not only enhance your email marketing efforts but also move one step closer to achieving financial freedom.

Automating Your Email Marketing

In the quest for financial freedom, effective time management is indispensable. Automating your email marketing is a pivotal strategy that can substantially increase your efficiency and earnings. Let's delve into the nuts and bolts of email automation and how it can serve as a powerful tool in your passive income arsenal.

To start with, the essence of email marketing is in building relationships. Your email list consists of people who are interested in your content, products, or services. They trust you enough to provide their email addresses, and that's no small feat. Automation ensures that you nurture these relationships without constant manual effort, allowing you to focus on building other income streams.

At its core, email automation involves setting up sequences that are triggered by specific actions. These triggers can be as simple as someone subscribing to your newsletter or as complex as tracking user behavior on your website. Once set up, these sequences run in the background, continuously engaging your audience and driving conversions.

Imagine the power of sending a welcome series to new subscribers. This sequence could include a greeting email, followed by emails introducing your best content, case studies, or success stories. Not only does this create a positive first impression, but it also sets the tone for future interactions. Each of these emails can be crafted once, refined over time, and sent to every new subscriber without additional effort on your part.

One of the most valuable aspects of email automation is segmentation. Segmentation allows you to tailor your messages to different segments of your audience, making your emails more relevant and effective. For instance, you can segment your list based on demographics, past purchase behavior, or engagement levels. A well-segmented email list ensures that you're sending the right message to the right people at the right time.

Consider your email marketing efforts similar to a garden. Automation is the irrigation system that ensures every plant gets the right amount of water, while segmentation is adjusting the flow based on individual plant needs. This strategy nurtures your "plants" into flourishing, loyal assets.

Automating email marketing includes not just sending emails but also following up. Follow-up sequences can help you stay top-of-mind and guide potential customers through the decision-making process. For instance, if someone abandons a shopping cart on your e-commerce site, an automated follow-up sequence could include a reminder email, a limited-time discount, and a final call-to-action.

Let's talk about tools. Numerous platforms like Mailchimp, ConvertKit, and ActiveCampaign offer robust automation features. These tools provide user-friendly interfaces to create and manage your email sequences, track analytics, and continuously optimize your campaigns. The beauty of these platforms is in their ability to integrate with other tools you might already be using, such as your website or CRM software.

Analytics play a crucial role in automated email marketing. Understanding open rates, click-through rates, and conversion rates can help you fine-tune your strategies. Most email marketing tools come with built-in analytics that provide insights into how well your sequences are performing. Use this data to make informed decisions and continually refine your approach.

Remember, the goal of email automation is not just to save time but to enhance the customer experience. An exceptional automated email sequence feels personal and timely to the recipient. Achieving this level of personalization requires thoughtful planning and regular updates. Consider incorporating personalized elements like the recipient's name, recommendations based on their behavior, or special offers tailored to their interests.

Automated email marketing also helps in scaling your efforts. As your subscriber list grows, manually managing email campaigns becomes impractical. Automation scales with you, allowing you to handle thousands of subscribers as easily as hundreds. This scalability is essential as it frees you up to explore other revenue-generating activities.

Additionally, automating your email marketing can significantly increase your return on investment (ROI). By consistently engaging your audience with relevant content and offers, you're more likely to see higher conversion rates. This translates to more sales, subscriptions, or whatever your desired outcome is, without adding to your workload.

Another benefit is consistency. With automation, you ensure that your audience receives communication at regular intervals. This consistency builds trust and keeps your brand at the forefront of their minds. Whether it's a weekly newsletter or a monthly product update, automation ensures that you never miss a beat.

Finally, don't underestimate the peace of mind that comes from knowing your email marketing is handled. The passive nature of automated email campaigns means you can focus on other important aspects of your business and personal life, confident that your email marketing is working seamlessly in the background.

To sum up, automating your email marketing is not just a smart strategy; it's a necessary step towards achieving financial freedom. It enables you to nurture relationships, segment your audience, follow up effectively, utilize powerful tools, leverage analytics, personalize communication, scale efforts, increase ROI, and maintain consistency—all with minimal manual effort. Embrace the power of email automation and watch your passive income streams flourish.

Chapter 12:
Advanced Passive Income Strategies

Building on foundational passive income concepts, let's explore advanced strategies that can elevate your financial game. Intellectual property licensing allows you to earn royalties from patents, trademarks, or creative works, creating a continuous stream of income from your ingenuity. Silent business partnerships enable you to earn a share of profits from businesses without active involvement, providing a lucrative yet hands-free revenue source. Additionally, high-yield savings accounts and peer-to-peer lending platforms offer ways to grow your savings with higher interest rates and returns compared to traditional banks. Mastering these strategies not only diversifies your income but also solidifies your path to financial independence, offering you the freedom to live life on your terms.

Intellectual Property Licensing

Moving beyond foundational passive income strategies, let's dive into the world of intellectual property licensing. Intellectual property (IP) refers to creations of the mind: inventions, literary and artistic works, symbols, names, and images used in commerce. It's powerful because it allows you to earn income from your creative endeavors by granting rights to others while retaining ownership.

Think about it: every time you come up with a unique idea, whether it's a catchy jingle, a groundbreaking invention, or an engaging book, you're creating intellectual property. Licensing is about allowing others to use that property under specific terms, typically in exchange for a fee or royalty. It's a win-win, as they get to leverage your creativity, and you get to earn passive income.

Consider some household names. The "Happy Birthday" song generated royalties for over a century before it entered the public domain. Patented inventions, like the first transistor radio or the Post-it note, also earned their creators significant returns through licensing agreements. These aren't isolated cases but represent a category of passive income that's often overlooked.

To leverage intellectual property licensing, you first need to understand what qualifies as IP. It can be broken down into several categories: patents, trademarks, copyrights, and trade secrets. Each category has its own set of rules and potential for income. A patent, for instance, gives you the exclusive right to an invention, while a copyright protects original works of authorship like music, books, and software.

Getting a patent is often a rigorous process involving legal and technical scrutiny, but the rewards can be substantial. For instance, if you invent a new type of medical device, you could license it to a manufacturing company. They produce and sell it, and you collect a percentage of every sale. You might even negotiate upfront payments to cover initial development costs. It's like planting a seed and watching it grow into a fruitful tree.

Trademarks, on the other hand, protect brand names, slogans, and logos. If you develop a unique and recognizable brand, you can license it to other businesses. Take the example of franchise models like McDonald's or Subway. Franchisees pay for the right to use the brand, ensuring consistency while generating passive income for the parent company.

Copyrights protect your original works like songs, books, apps, and educational courses. Imagine you're an author who writes a popular novel. Beyond direct sales, you could license rights for film adaptations, audiobooks, or translations. Each license is an additional income stream stemming from a single creative effort.

Trade secrets are another valuable asset. These include formulas, practices, designs, or compilation of information not known to the public and provide a business advantage. While trade secrets aren't typically "licensed" in the traditional sense, controlling access and usage through confidentiality agreements can be lucrative as well.

To successfully license your IP, start by protecting it legally. Patents, copyrights, and trademarks all require legal registration and sometimes ongoing fees. A registered trademark, for instance, is more credible and defensible in court. The initial investment is a form of due diligence that pays off in the long run.

Next, identify potential licensees—businesses or individuals who can benefit from using your IP. This means understanding market needs and targeting entities whose goals align with your product. For example, if you've designed an innovative educational software, seeking out schools, educational institutions, or tech companies makes sense.

Negotiation skills are crucial here. Licensing agreements should be mutually beneficial, clearly outlining terms like usage rights, duration, territorial limitations, and compensation. A well-crafted agreement protects both parties and ensures that your IP remains an ongoing source of passive income.

Royalty structures are commonly used in licensing deals. These agreements specify that you earn a percentage of revenue from the product or service that uses your IP. The percentage can vary widely depending on the industry, the IP's perceived value, and market trends.

For instance, software licenses might command lower percentages but generate high volumes, while niche patents might fetch higher per-unit royalties.

If an upfront fee is included, you can cover some or all initial costs, making this income stream even more attractive. This initial influx can then be reinvested into other passive income strategies, creating a reinforcing cycle of financial growth.

The digital age offers even more opportunities for intellectual property licensing. Online platforms simplify connecting content creators with users. Websites like Shutterstock allow photographers to license their images, while digital marketplaces such as Envato enable designers to sell templates and graphics. These platforms act as intermediaries, taking a cut but providing exposure and easing administrative burdens.

Leveraging intellectual property licensing isn't a passive income strategy where you can set it and forget it. Regularly reviewing agreements, keeping up with industry trends, and maintaining legal protections are all part of a dynamic process. However, the rewards can be substantial and long-lasting, making it a crucial piece in your passive income portfolio.

When you think about financial freedom, intellectual property licensing opens up avenues limited only by your creativity and ambition. It's about taking the ideas, hard work, and creativity you've already invested in and transforming them into ongoing revenue streams. With focus, legal backing, and strategic partnerships, licensing your intellectual property can be a game-changing strategy on your journey to financial independence.

Silent Business Partnerships

When we talk about advanced passive income strategies, one gem that often flies under the radar is silent business partnerships. The concept is straightforward but incredibly powerful: you invest in a business and share in the profits, without having to actively manage or even get involved in the day-to-day operations. This section will delve deep into how silent business partnerships can become a cornerstone of your passive income portfolio.

First off, what exactly does a silent business partnership entail? Simply put, a silent partner provides capital to a business venture but doesn't have a role in the operations or management of the business. This is a win-win situation: the active partners get the funds they need to grow the business, while silent partners earn a return on their investment without the hassle of running the business themselves.

The allure of being a silent partner is clear—you can potentially earn substantial income without lifting more than the pen you used to sign the partnership agreement. It's the epitome of passive income, yet it requires due diligence upfront to ensure your investment is well-placed. Think of it this way: just as you wouldn't buy a rental property in a declining neighborhood, you shouldn't invest in a business without thoroughly vetting it first.

So, how do you identify suitable opportunities for silent partnerships? Start by leveraging your existing network. Often, the best opportunities are right under your nose. Do you know someone who's passionate about their business but needs some financial backing to take it to the next level? Also, be on the lookout for businesses showing consistent growth, have a solid business model, and are led by trustworthy and competent individuals.

Another important aspect is understanding the legal framework. Silent business partnerships are usually formalized through legal agreements that outline the terms of the partnership, including profit-sharing ratios, your rights as a silent partner, and the exit strategy. Consulting with a business attorney can save you from potential pitfalls and ensure you're protected.

Don't underestimate the power of diversification within your portfolio of silent partnerships. Just as you wouldn't invest all your savings into one stock, spreading your investments across different businesses can mitigate risks. For instance, consider allocating funds across sectors such as technology, retail, and food services. This diversified approach not only reduces risk but can also capitalize on the unique growth opportunities in different markets.

The financial returns from silent partnerships can be compelling. Unlike traditional investments like stocks or bonds that typically offer single-digit percentage returns, a successful business can generate much higher profit margins. However, it's crucial to have realistic expectations. While silent partnerships can yield impressive returns, the inherent risks mean that not every venture will be a home run.

Time and again, silence in these partnerships becomes golden as you trust the active partners to steer the business. It's important to stay informed about the business's performance through regular updates and reports. This can be facilitated by setting clear communication guidelines in the partnership agreement. Getting these updates ensures you remain connected with how your money is working for you.

There's an educational component to this as well. By engaging in silent partnerships, you get to peek under the hood of various industries and business models. This experiential learning can be invaluable as you continue to grow and diversify your passive income streams. It's like getting a mini-MBA without ever stepping into a classroom.

Tax implications are another critical area to consider. Silent partnerships can provide certain tax benefits, such as deductions for business expenses. However, you'll need to be aware of how partnership income is taxed in your jurisdiction, as tax laws can be complex and vary widely. Professional advice from a tax consultant can help you navigate these waters efficiently.

Exit strategies are just as important as entry strategies. Before committing your capital, discuss potential exit plans with the active partners. Whether it's selling your share back to them, selling to a third party, or even liquidating the business, having a clear exit strategy ensures you have options if circumstances change.

Trust is an intangible yet critical element in silent partnerships. The success of your investment hinges largely on the honesty, integrity, and competence of the active partners. This is why due diligence is non-negotiable. Take the time to meet the team, understand their vision, and get a feel for their commitment and work ethic.

Silent partnerships can also serve as a springboard for more active forms of investment if you ever choose to get involved. As you gain more confidence and insight, you might decide to take a more hands-on role in other ventures. But for now, the passive nature of silent partnerships makes them an ideal option for those looking to dip their toes without diving into the deep end.

In sum, silent business partnerships provide a compelling opportunity to grow your passive income streams. They blend the potential for high returns with minimal involvement, offering a balanced approach to income generation. As with all investments, the keys to success lie in thorough research, diversified portfolio management, and clear legal agreements.

If financial freedom is your goal, adding silent business partnerships to your strategy could be the move that helps you break free from the 9-to-5 grind. It's an invitation to let your money work harder for you, achieving greater returns while you enjoy the freedom and flexibility that come with true passive income.

High-Yield Savings and Peer-to-Peer Lending

In the quest for financial freedom, two often overlooked yet powerful strategies are high-yield savings accounts and peer-to-peer (P2P) lending platforms. Both offer a blend of low to moderate risk with the potential for reasonable returns, making them apt choices for a diversified portfolio aimed at generating passive income.

Firstly, let's delve into high-yield savings accounts. These are essentially savings accounts offered by banks or credit unions that pay significantly higher interest rates compared to traditional savings accounts. Their appeal lies in their simplicity and safety. Backed by the Federal Deposit Insurance Corporation (FDIC) or the National Credit Union Administration (NCUA), these accounts provide a secure harbor for your money with virtually no risk of loss.

One of the main advantages of high-yield savings accounts is liquidity. You can access your funds easily, allowing you to maintain a safety net for emergencies while still earning interest. This makes high-yield savings accounts a strategic component of an overall passive income plan, providing both stability and flexibility.

To maximize the benefits of high-yield savings accounts, it's important to shop around. Online banks often offer the highest rates since they have lower overhead costs compared to their brick-and-mortar counterparts. Some institutions also offer promotional rates for new customers, which can further boost your earnings. A few hours of research can result in a significantly better yield on your savings.

High-yield savings accounts won't make you rich overnight, but they're an excellent way to earn more from the money you need to keep liquid. Whether you're saving for a down payment on a property, an emergency fund, or simply looking for a set-and-forget investment option, the interest accrued from these accounts adds up over time, contributing to your overall financial health.

Now, let's shift gears and explore peer-to-peer lending. P2P lending platforms like LendingClub, Prosper, and others connect individual lenders with borrowers, cutting out traditional banks. This model benefits both parties: borrowers often get better rates than they would from banks, while lenders can earn higher returns compared to traditional savings or investment accounts.

As an investor, P2P lending allows you to diversify your portfolio with relatively small amounts of money. Most platforms let you start lending with as little as $25 per loan, spreading your risk over multiple loans. The returns typically range from 5% to 12%, depending on the borrower's creditworthiness and the term of the loan.

However, with the higher potential returns come higher risks. Unlike high-yield savings accounts, P2P lending is not insured, meaning that if a borrower defaults, you could lose your investment. It's crucial to approach P2P lending with a strategy. One effective method is to diversify widely: by investing small amounts in many loans, you mitigate the impact of a single default.

Many platforms offer automated investing features that align with your risk tolerance, automatically selecting and funding loans based on your criteria. This can save you time and help ensure that your investment is spread across a wide array of borrowers. The key is to balance risk with reward, understanding that higher returns often involve higher risks.

Another advantage of P2P lending is the relatively steady income stream it can generate. Borrowers make monthly payments that include both principal and interest, providing a regular cash flow. This can be particularly appealing if you're looking to supplement your passive income without needing to sell off investments or touch your savings.

Incorporating P2P lending into your passive income strategy also allows you to invest in people and projects that resonate with you. Many platforms provide detailed profiles of borrowers, letting you choose loans that align with your interests or values. This adds a personal touch to your investment, potentially making the process more rewarding on a personal level.

However, it's essential to keep an eye on fees. P2P platforms typically charge a service fee, which can eat into your returns. Be sure to read the fine print and understand all the costs involved before committing your money. It's equally vital to regularly review your P2P portfolio, reinvesting payments, and adjusting your strategy as needed.

Both high-yield savings accounts and P2P lending contribute to a well-rounded passive income plan. The former offers security and liquidity, while the latter provides the potential for higher returns, albeit with increased risk. By integrating both into your financial strategy, you can achieve a balance that aligns with your risk tolerance and financial goals.

Consider high-yield savings accounts as your financial foundation—a stable, low-risk way to grow your money. On the other hand, think of P2P lending as an opportunity to reach for higher returns while helping individuals and small businesses achieve their financial goals. Together, they form a powerful duo in the landscape of advanced passive income strategies.

As you progress on your journey towards financial freedom, the key is diversification and informed decision-making. High-yield savings and P2P lending are but two tools in your arsenal, but they can play pivotal roles in creating sustainable and diversified income streams. Take the time to understand each option, weigh their pros and cons, and incorporate them wisely into your overall strategy. Financial freedom is not a distant dream; it becomes a reality through informed choices and diverse investments.

Next, we'll explore other advanced passive income strategies, delving deeper into intellectual property licensing and silent business partnerships. Each avenue offers unique opportunities to build and sustain your wealth. Stay focused, stay informed, and keep moving forward. Your journey to financial independence continues!

Chapter 13:
Scaling and Optimizing Your Passive Income

You've laid the groundwork, created multiple streams, and now it's time to scale and optimize your passive income. The key to scaling lies in diversification strategies, ensuring you aren't reliant on a single income stream that could dry up. This means spreading your investments, experimenting with new niches, and even breaking into different markets. Additionally, analyze and reinvest your profits wisely. By constantly assessing your income sources and reinvesting your gains, you can create a compounding effect that magnifies returns over time. Outsourcing and automation are equally crucial. By delegating tasks to experts and leveraging technology, you free up your time, allowing for more strategic planning and growth. Remember, the journey doesn't end at creating passive income—scaling and optimizing is where you transition from sustenance to abundance, making your financial freedom not just a distant dream but a tangible reality.

diversification strategies

When it comes to scaling and optimizing your passive income, diversification should be one of your cornerstone strategies. At its core, diversification means spreading your investments across multiple income streams to minimize risk and increase the potential for returns.

Relying on just one source of passive income can be risky—and that's why diversifying is crucial for achieving true financial freedom.

The beauty of diversification lies in its ability to stabilize your income. Imagine you've invested solely in rental properties, and an economic downturn hits the real estate market. If you don't have other income sources, you're vulnerable. By contrast, if you've also got investments in dividend-paying stocks, digital product sales, and perhaps even some affiliate marketing, you're much more likely to ride out any turbulence unscathed.

Diversifying isn't just about reducing risk—it's also about opening up new avenues for growth. Think of it as planting multiple seeds in different types of soil. Some might sprout quicker than others, but the overall garden will flourish over time. This varied approach gives you multiple opportunities to explore and leverage, amplifying your overall wealth-building efforts.

Real estate often serves as a foundational passive income stream for many investors. However, owning properties isn't limited to traditional rental income. You might also diversify within real estate by incorporating different strategies like real estate investment trusts (REITs) or even short-term rentals through platforms like Airbnb. Each of these avenues operates differently and possesses its own set of strengths and weaknesses, allowing you to balance risk and reward.

Digital products are another viable component of a diversified portfolio. With today's technology, creating and selling digital items—like eBooks, online courses, or software—has become easier than ever. These products come with the appealing advantage of low ongoing costs, making them highly scalable. Plus, they allow for creative expression and thought leadership in your field, which can build your brand and influence.

Stock market investing introduces you to dividends, a straightforward way to generate passive income. However, the stock market isn't monolithic; you can diversify within it by investing in individual stocks, exchange-traded funds (ETFs), and mutual funds. Each has its own benefits and considerations, helping you mitigate the risks associated with market volatility.

Affiliate marketing offers yet another diversification route. As you build out affiliate websites and create content aimed at driving traffic, you can tap into multiple niches. By doing so, you shield yourself from sector-specific downturns. For instance, if one product category underperforms, the success of another can help offset any financial setbacks.

Don't overlook e-commerce and dropshipping as powerful diversification pathways. Setting up an online store allows you to explore various product offerings and supplier relationships. Automating order fulfillment ensures that your time investment remains minimal, freeing you up to focus on other income-generating activities.

Blogging not only allows you to share your expertise but also provides multiple revenue streams, from advertising to sponsored content. Your blog can serve as a hub for all your other ventures, tying them together into a cohesive, diversified income-generating machine.

Social media platforms like YouTube and Instagram offer monetization opportunities that range from ad revenues to influencer partnerships. Each platform has its own set of algorithms and audience engagement rules, offering unique challenges and rewards. Engaging on multiple social media fronts can significantly broaden your income base.

Email marketing remains one of the most effective tools for driving sustained engagement and sales. By diversifying your approach to email marketing—through various campaigns, automated funnels, and lead magnets—you can maximize the impact and reliability of this income stream.

Advanced strategies such as intellectual property licensing, silent business partnerships, and peer-to-peer lending can further diversify your income. These may require more sophisticated planning and legal considerations but serve to solidify your portfolio's overall resilience.

Diversification doesn't just happen at the macro level of choosing different income streams; it also happens within each stream. For instance, within stock market investments, you might hold a mix of dividend aristocrats, growth stocks, and international equities. In digital products, you could diversify by creating multiple items targeted at different audience segments.

As you diversify, you'll also want to continually analyze and reinvest your profits to fuel further growth. This reinvestment strategy could involve pumping money back into your most successful ventures or seeding new, promising ones. Think of reinvestment as the water and nutrients that sustain your growing garden.

Outsourcing and automation are pivotal for managing a diversified portfolio effectively. Once different streams are set up, you'll need systems in place to keep them running smoothly with minimal manual intervention. Tools and specialized contractors can help manage various aspects, freeing you to focus on high-level strategy and scaling.

Ultimately, diversification is about safeguarding against uncertainty while seizing as many opportunities as possible. It's a dynamic, ongoing process requiring regular assessment and adjustment. As markets evolve and your understanding deepens, your diversified portfolio will be well-positioned to grow and adapt, leading you ever closer to financial freedom.

Analyzing and Reinvesting Profits

As you begin to see the fruits of your passive income endeavors, it's crucial to not only savor those early successes but also to smartly analyze and reinvest your profits. This step is paramount in scaling and optimizing your income streams to achieve long-term financial freedom.

First, you need to analyze your profits comprehensively. This means not just looking at the amount of money coming in but understanding where it's coming from, what strategies are working, and which areas may need improvement. You should break down your income sources and evaluate each one on key performance indicators such as return on investment (ROI), growth potential, and stability.

Let's take an example: suppose you have multiple income streams from blogging, rental properties, and dividend stocks. Assess the performance of each stream by looking at the income generated versus the effort expended and the initial and ongoing investments required. By doing so, you can identify which sources are the most efficient and which ones might be draining resources.

Next, it's vital to automate this process as much as possible. Utilize accounting software and financial dashboards that offer real-time data and insights. These tools can help track your multiple income streams and provide regular reports that make the analysis straightforward and routine.

After analyzing where your money is going and what it is accomplishing, it's time to make strategic decisions about reinvesting your profits. Reinvestment is the linchpin of scaling up your passive income. By allocating your profits back into your ventures—be it purchasing additional rental properties, expanding your blog's reach, or buying more dividend-paying stocks—you are planting seeds for exponential growth.

One common strategy is to reinvest a percentage of your profits. For instance, you could decide to reinvest 70% of your earnings while keeping the remaining 30% as liquid assets or for personal use. This balance allows you to grow your income streams without overextending yourself financially.

Consider diversification as a critical element of reinvestment. Diversification reduces risk and increases the potential for returns across different markets and asset classes. If your profits are largely coming from one investment, such as rental properties, think about diversifying into other areas like digital products or stock dividends to spread the risk and enhance growth opportunities.

Keep in mind that reinvesting your profits isn't just about where you put your money; it's also about how you optimize your existing income streams. Sometimes, rather than diversifying, doubling down on what's already working can yield significant returns. This might involve investing in better marketing for your blog, purchasing more efficient property management software, or acquiring premium tools to enhance your digital products.

Another vital aspect of reinvesting profits is seeking professional advice. Financial advisors and investment experts can offer invaluable insights into how to best allocate your profits. They can help you navigate complex financial landscapes, identify lucrative opportunities, and avoid common pitfalls.

Mentorship and learning from those who have successfully scaled their passive income streams can also offer practical insights. Engage with communities, attend seminars, or participate in online forums where you can gain knowledge from those who've walked this path before you. Their experiences and strategies can provide a blueprint for your journey.

Furthermore, keep track of your investments and recalibrate as needed. The financial world is dynamic, and what works today might not work tomorrow. Regularly revisit your investments, reevaluate their performance, and be prepared to pivot if necessary. Staying adaptable will ensure sustained growth and mitigate risks.

Your mindset plays a crucial role in this phase. Embrace a growth-oriented mentality, where every dollar earned is seen as a potential catalyst for further earnings. This shift from a consumption mindset to a reinvestment mindset can accelerate your journey towards financial independence.

Understand that reinvesting profits isn't just a financial decision; it's a commitment to your long-term vision. Financial freedom is achieved through consistent, strategic efforts. Every choice you make today sets the stage for your future success.

Lastly, celebrate small wins and milestones along the way. Recognizing and rewarding your progress keeps you motivated and aligned with your long-term goals. It could be as simple as rewarding yourself with a small luxury or merely acknowledging how far you've come.

Analyzing and reinvesting your profits is a dynamic process that requires vigilance, strategy, and adaptability. By carefully evaluating your income streams and making informed reinvestments, you're significantly enhancing your ability to scale and optimize your passive income, moving steadily towards the ultimate goal—financial freedom.

Outsourcing and Automation

As you move forward in scaling and optimizing your passive income streams, it's crucial to understand the role of outsourcing and automation. These powerful tools not only free up your time but also allow you to leverage the expertise of others, ensuring that your income streams grow and function efficiently without your constant involvement.

First, let's discuss outsourcing. At its core, outsourcing is all about delegating tasks that are either outside your skill set or that consume too much of your time. This delegation can significantly speed up your business growth by enabling you to focus on high-impact activities. Think about it: do you really need to be tweaking your website's design or responding to every customer service email? Probably not. Delegate those tasks so you can concentrate on what truly matters, like strategizing new income streams or optimizing existing ones.

One of the best places to start with outsourcing is identifying what tasks are essential but repetitive. Common candidates include administrative tasks, customer service, social media management, and even content creation. Platforms like Upwork, Freelancer, and Fiverr have made it easier than ever to find skilled freelancers who can handle these responsibilities, allowing you to focus on the bigger picture.

When outsourcing, clarity is paramount. Ensure you set clear expectations, deadlines, and deliverables. Clear communication will improve the quality of the work you receive and will make your collaboration smoother. Craft detailed job descriptions and use project management tools like Asana or Trello to keep track of tasks and progress.

Now, let's turn to automation. Automation is about setting up systems that can operate on their own, minimizing the need for human intervention. Think about email marketing campaigns that send pre-written messages based on customer actions, or e-commerce stores that automate order processing and fulfillment. Automating these areas can create a self-sustaining system, eliminating tedious tasks and reducing the chance of errors.

The key to effective automation is selecting the right tools. For email marketing, platforms like Mailchimp, ConvertKit, and ActiveCampaign offer robust automation features that can cater to most needs. For managing social media, tools such as Hootsuite and Buffer can help schedule posts across various platforms, keeping your audience engaged without you having to lift a finger daily.

Automation isn't just about saving time; it's also about consistency. For example, if you're running an affiliate marketing blog, consistently publishing content is crucial. Using automation tools, you can schedule posts in advance, ensuring that fresh content is always available to your readers, even when you're busy with other tasks.

It's essential to strike a balance between automation and personalization. Automation can handle repetitive tasks, but some aspects of your business might still require a personal touch. For instance, customer service issues can generally be handled through automated responses, but more complex problems will likely need human intervention. Make sure your systems allow for this flexibility.

Your financial analytics can also be automated. Tools like QuickBooks and Xero can automate bookkeeping tasks, generate financial reports, and even remind you about tax deadlines. This not only saves time but also helps in maintaining accuracy and reducing the risk of oversight.

Security is another vital consideration when automating. Ensure that the tools you're using comply with data protection regulations and have strong security measures in place. The last thing you want is to compromise your business's integrity and customer trust.

One excellent example of combining outsourcing and automation is in the realm of digital products. Let's say you've created an online course. You can outsource the creation of promotional materials to a professional designer while automating your email marketing to nurture leads and convert them into paying customers. This holistic approach ensures your product reaches a broader audience without additional manual effort from you.

Remember, both outsourcing and automation are investments. While they do require an initial outlay, the return on investment can be substantial. Time saved and efficiency gained will far outweigh the costs, allowing you to scale your passive income streams faster and more effectively.

One common misconception is that outsourcing and automation are only for large enterprises. In reality, they are crucial for businesses of all sizes, especially for solo entrepreneurs and small businesses. By leveraging these tools, you can punch above your weight and compete with bigger players, all while maintaining a lean operation.

As you integrate outsourcing and automation into your various passive income streams, continuously monitor and optimize these systems. Regularly review performance metrics and make adjustments as needed. Remember, the goal is to create a business environment where everything runs smoothly and efficiently, freeing you up to explore new opportunities and enjoy the fruits of your labor.

To wrap up, the journey towards scaling and optimizing your passive income is made significantly more achievable through strategic outsourcing and robust automation. These aren't just optional enhancements; they are essential elements in your toolkit, allowing you to build a scalable, sustainable business model that requires minimal day-to-day involvement from you.

By mastering these strategies, you gain the freedom to focus on what truly matters – whether that's expanding new ventures, spending time with loved ones, or simply enjoying the financial freedom you've worked so hard to achieve. Now go out there and make it happen!

Chapter 14:
The Legalities of Passive Income

Navigating the waters of passive income isn't just about clever investments or building successful ventures; it's equally crucial to understand the legal landscape to protect your hard-earned assets and ensure compliance. Establishing the right business structure—be it an LLC, S-Corp, or sole proprietorship—can significantly affect your tax obligations and liability exposure. Understanding the tax implications and ensuring you meet all compliance requirements is not just a good practice; it's essential for long-term success and peace of mind. Additionally, safeguarding your assets through proper legal channels, like trademarks and copyrights, can shield you from unforeseen legal disputes that could jeopardize your financial freedom. By focusing on these key legal aspects, you lay down a robust foundation that supports the sustained growth of your passive income streams, allowing you the freedom to focus on scaling and optimizing your ventures without unnecessary distractions.

Setting Up the Right Business Structure

As you step into the world of passive income, setting up the right business structure can make or break your journey. It's more than just a legal formality—it's the backbone that supports your financial freedom. Choosing the correct structure isn't always straightforward, but it's crucial for minimizing taxes, limiting liability, and maximizing your income.

First things first, you need to recognize that there isn't a one-size-fits-all answer. Your ideal business structure depends on various factors like the nature of your passive income streams, your risk tolerance, and even your long-term goals. You'll mostly have options like sole proprietorships, partnerships, limited liability companies (LLCs), and corporations. Each has its pros and cons, so let's dive into those.

Sole Proprietorship: Simplicity and Control

If you're just dipping your toes into passive income, a sole proprietorship might seem attractive due to its simplicity. There's minimal paperwork, and you have complete control. However, simplicity comes at a price. The downside? There's no separation between you and your business. If your business faces financial trouble or legal issues, your personal assets are at risk.

Partnership: Sharing the Load

Partnerships can be great for those who are venturing into passive income with a friend or business partner. You get to share the workload and pool resources, making it easier to scale your operations. The catch? Just like sole proprietorships, partnerships generally don't shield you from personal liability. Plus, conflicts between partners can complicate decision-making and disrupt your business.

LLC: The Best of Both Worlds

A Limited Liability Company, or LLC, often provides a balanced blend of simplicity and protection. Unlike a sole proprietorship or partnership, an LLC separates your personal and business liabilities, meaning your personal assets are generally protected if things go south. Tax-wise, LLCs offer flexibility; you can choose to be taxed as a sole proprietorship, partnership, or corporation.

Forming an LLC requires more paperwork and costs compared to a sole proprietorship, but the benefits often outweigh these initial hurdles. This structure is especially beneficial for real estate investments, digital product sales, and other significant passive income ventures.

Corporation: For the Long Haul

If you're thinking big and aiming to scale your passive income streams into a substantial enterprise, a corporation might be your best bet. Corporations offer the strongest protection for personal assets and make it easier to raise capital. You also get perpetual existence, meaning your business can continue even if you decide to step down.

However, corporations come with complex regulations and are subject to double taxation—first on corporate profits and again on dividends distributed to shareholders. This downside can be mitigated through an S Corporation election, which allows profits to pass through to your personal tax return, avoiding double taxation.

Legal and Accounting Guidance

It's pivotal to consult with legal and accounting experts when setting up your business structure. They can provide tailored advice based on your unique situation and objectives. Skipping this step could cost you more in the long run, not just in terms of money, but also time and peace of mind.

Compliance and Record-Keeping

Once you've selected a structure, the journey doesn't end there. Maintaining compliance with local, state, and federal regulations is non-negotiable. Regular record-keeping is essential, and while it may seem tedious, it's crucial for financial transparency and legal protection.

Platforms like QuickBooks or Wave can simplify this process, allowing you to automate much of your bookkeeping and focus on growing your passive income streams. Trust me, when tax season rolls around, you'll be glad you kept everything organized.

Beyond mere compliance, keeping detailed records helps you analyze which passive income streams are most profitable. This insight enables you to make informed decisions about where to invest your time and resources next.

Future-Proofing Your Business

As your passive income empire grows, you may find that your initial business structure no longer fits your needs. Don't be afraid to evolve. Transitioning from an LLC to a corporation, for instance, might make sense if you're scaling rapidly and need to attract investors.

Be proactive about anticipating these changes. Regularly review your business structure, especially as new opportunities or challenges arise. Flexibility isn't just a buzzword; it's a necessity for long-term success.

Leveraging Tax Benefits

Each business structure comes with its own tax benefits and obligations. For example, owning rental properties through an LLC can offer significant tax deductions for expenses like maintenance, property management fees, and depreciation. A corporation can provide fringe benefits like health insurance and retirement plans, which can be highly advantageous.

Utilize these benefits to your advantage. Work with a tax advisor to identify opportunities for tax savings and ensure you're not leaving money on the table. Efficient tax planning can significantly boost your overall profitability.

Choosing the right business structure is a strategic decision that can set the tone for your entire passive income journey. It's the foundation on which you'll build your empire, so take the time to get it right. With the proper guidance and a clear understanding of your options, you'll be well on your way to achieving financial freedom and long-term success.

Understanding Taxes and Compliance

When it comes to passive income, understanding taxes and compliance is crucial. It's easy to get caught up in the excitement of creating new revenue streams and forget about the legal obligations that come with them. But trust me, skipping out on this part can lead to some serious headaches down the line. So let's deep dive into the nitty-gritty and break down what you need to know.

First off, it's essential to distinguish between active and passive income for tax purposes. The IRS treats these types of income differently, and your tax responsibilities will vary accordingly. Active income generally refers to wages, salaries, and tips—money you actively work to earn. On the other hand, passive income typically comes from investments or business ventures in which you're not actively involved.

For example, rental income from a property you own is considered passive, as is the income you earn from dividends or interest. Yet, the IRS has specific guidelines that define what constitutes passive income, and these rules can influence your tax obligations significantly. Thus, it's advisable to consult a tax professional to fully understand how your specific passive income streams will be categorized.

Now, let's talk about tax rates. Passive income can be taxed at different rates compared to active income, and these rates can influence your strategy. Capital gains tax, for instance, is often lower than the ordinary income tax rate, particularly if you hold your investments for over a year. Understanding these rates can help you plan for tax-efficient investment strategies, ensuring you keep more of your hard-earned money.

In terms of real estate, rental income is not only taxable but also often allows for some beneficial deductions. Mortgage interest, property taxes, and even depreciation can significantly reduce your taxable rental income. Yet, these deductions come with their own set of rules and requirements, so make sure you're keeping thorough records.

For those creating digital products, such as eBooks or online courses, sales can generate significant passive income. But, don't forget that this income is also subject to taxes. Online sellers often need to account for sales tax, depending on where their customers are located. Using platforms that handle sales tax can save you a lot of administrative headaches.

When investing in the stock market, be mindful of how dividends are taxed. Qualified dividends generally enjoy a lower tax rate compared to ordinary income, while non-qualified dividends do not. Understanding this distinction can influence which stocks you choose and how you structure your portfolio.

Another vehicle for passive income, affiliate marketing, brings its own tax considerations. Income generated from affiliate marketing is usually considered self-employment income, subjecting you to both income tax and self-employment tax. Keeping accurate records of your earnings and expenses is crucial to manage your tax liabilities effectively.

Compliance isn't just about taxes; it's also about adhering to relevant regulations that govern your passive income activities. For real estate, this might mean tenant rights laws and landlord responsibilities. For selling digital products or running an e-commerce store, it could mean data protection regulations and consumer rights.

Moreover, international investments and income streams from abroad add another layer of complexity. The U.S. has agreements with many countries to avoid double taxation, but this area can get complicated quickly. Tax professionals specializing in international tax law can provide invaluable insights and help ensure you're compliant.

Aside from federal taxes, don't forget about state and local tax obligations. Each state has its own tax laws, and municipalities may have additional requirements. Property taxes, sales taxes, and state income taxes can all impact your passive income and need to be accounted for in your financial planning.

Automating your taxes and compliance can be a game-changer. Many software solutions exist to help you track, categorize, and report your income and expenses. Leveraging technology can help you stay organized, ensure compliance, and ultimately save you time and money.

Finally, be proactive about your tax planning. Don't wait until the last minute to consult with tax professionals. Regularly reviewing your financials and tax obligations can help you make informed decisions and avoid any unpleasant surprises come tax season.

To wrap this up, understanding taxes and compliance might not be the most exciting part of building passive income, but it is indispensable for long-term success. The more you educate yourself, leverage professional advice, and utilize technology, the more effectively you can manage your tax obligations. This ensures that your passive income streams remain not just profitable but sustainable, paving the way for lasting financial freedom.

Protecting Your Assets

Creating passive income streams is an incredibly rewarding journey, but to truly reap the benefits, you must protect the assets you accumulate along the way. Protecting your assets is not just about safeguarding your money—it's about securing your future, ensuring the longevity of your financial success, and mitigating risks that could potentially derail your journey toward financial freedom.

First things first, you need to understand the importance of separating your personal and business finances. This is a foundational step often overlooked by beginners. Mixing personal and business finances can lead to a host of legal complications and make you more vulnerable to liabilities. Setting up a legal entity, like an LLC (Limited Liability Company), can provide a shield between your personal assets and your business activities. An LLC also offers flexibility in taxation, making it a smart choice for many entrepreneurs.

Once you've established a legal entity, scaling your business becomes less risky, but it's crucial to continuously evaluate and adjust your asset protection strategies. As you diversify your passive income streams—from real estate to digital products—each one will come with its unique set of risks. Understanding and addressing these risks at each stage will go a long way in protecting your assets.

Insurance is another critical component of asset protection. Whether it's property insurance for your real estate investments, liability insurance for your business operations, or cybersecurity insurance for your digital ventures, these protective measures are essential. They may seem like unnecessary expenses at first, but insurance serves as a safety net that can save you from catastrophic losses.

Think about the concept of risk management. This isn't just a buzzword; it's a practice that the wealthiest and most successful individuals and corporations swear by. Regularly revisiting and updating your insurance policies, risk management plans, and legal arrangements will help ensure that your assets remain protected as your passive income streams grow.

Legal compliance should never be an afterthought. Different types of passive income will require you to comply with different laws and regulations. Whether it's tax laws, zoning laws for real estate, or intellectual property laws for digital products, staying compliant can save you from hefty fines and legal battles. Establishing a relationship with a qualified attorney and accountant can offer the guidance necessary to navigate these complexities effectively.

Taxation is another crucial area that can impact your assets significantly. Avoiding tax pitfalls by understanding your tax obligations and taking advantage of tax benefits is key. For instance, certain investments may offer tax deferrals or deductions. A qualified tax advisor can help you identify and leverage these benefits, ensuring you're not leaving money on the table.

Don't overlook the value of an estate plan, especially if you're building substantial assets. Estate planning isn't just for the ultra-wealthy; it's a crucial tool for anyone looking to pass on their wealth efficiently and in accordance with their wishes. This includes setting up trusts, designating beneficiaries, and drafting a will to ensure your assets are allocated correctly.

Another essential aspect of asset protection is confidentiality. The less information malicious parties have about your assets, the better. Using trusts or other legal structures can help keep your asset information private, making it more difficult for potential lawsuits or creditors to target them.

Your digital assets also need protection. With the increasing reliance on digital platforms for passive income, safeguarding your online properties through strong cybersecurity practices is paramount. Regularly updating software, using strong, unique passwords, and employing two-factor authentication are simple yet effective ways to enhance your digital security.

Let's talk about diversification. This isn't just a strategy for maximizing returns but also a means of reducing risk. Diversifying your passive income streams—across different asset types, industries, and geographical locations—ensures that a downturn in one area doesn't significantly impact your overall financial health.

Automation can also play a role in asset protection. Automating payments, invoicing, and even some investment management tasks reduces the risk of human error and creates a consistent, reliable system for managing your finances.

The importance of regular audits and reviews cannot be overstated. Whether it's financial audits, software security checks, or legal compliance reviews, these periodic examinations help identify vulnerabilities and ensure that your asset protection strategies remain robust and effective.

Lastly, always stay educated. The financial world is dynamic, with laws, risks, and opportunities evolving continuously. Commit to lifelong learning—read books, take courses, and attend seminars on asset protection and financial management. Being proactive about your education will empower you to make informed decisions, keeping your assets secure and your financial future bright.

In essence, protecting your assets isn't a one-time task but an ongoing process. It involves being proactive, staying informed, and regularly revisiting your strategies to adapt to new challenges and opportunities. By doing so, you'll not only safeguard what you've worked hard to build but also ensure a more stable and successful journey toward financial freedom.

Chapter 15:
Addressing Common Challenges

Navigating the journey to financial freedom by building multiple streams of passive income isn't without its hurdles, but overcoming these challenges is key to long-term success. One of the most critical aspects is managing cash flow, ensuring that your passive income streams are sufficient to cover your expenses and allowing for reinvestment. Dealing with failures and setbacks is another common challenge; it's important to view them as learning opportunities and not deterrents. Ensuring the sustainability of your passive income requires ongoing attention and adaptation, whether it's updating your digital products or keeping up with real estate market trends. By proactively addressing these challenges, you can maintain and grow your income streams, ultimately achieving financial security and independence.

Managing Cash Flow

When it comes to creating and sustaining multiple streams of passive income, managing cash flow is one of the most critical aspects you'll need to master. Imagine cash flow as the lifeblood of your financial ventures. It keeps everything running smoothly, and without proper attention, even the most promising income streams can dry up and wither. So, let's delve into how you can take control of your cash flow and keep it steady, no matter what challenges arise.

First things first, understanding what cash flow actually means in the context of passive income is essential. Cash flow refers to the movement of money in and out of your assets. While income streams can vary in consistency and size, the goal is to have more money flowing in than out. Sounds simple, right? But the execution requires a strategic approach.

Your initial step should be to assess your current financial landscape. Know exactly what's coming in and what's going out. This might sound tedious, but trust me, it's crucial. Break down each passive income source and track its performance. Is your real estate investment bringing in steady rent payments? Are your eBooks and online courses consistent in generating sales? Understanding these metrics will give you the data you need to make informed decisions.

Once you've got a clear picture, you can start budgeting. Budgeting provides a solid foundation to manage cash flow effectively. Allocate portions of your earnings to cover recurring expenses, reinvestment opportunities, and of course, savings. The key here is to be realistic and conservative in your estimates. An unexpected drop in income or a sudden expense can strain your cash flow if you're not prepared.

Don't underestimate the power of diversification. Multiple passive income streams act as a buffer against the volatility of any single source. For instance, if one of your rental properties requires significant maintenance, the income from your online courses or stock dividends can keep you afloat. Diversification spreads out your risk and ensures you're not putting all your eggs in one basket.

Automating your financial processes can save you time and mental energy. Set up automatic transfers to savings accounts, schedule regular payments for recurring bills, and use financial software to keep track of your income and expenses. Automation eliminates the risk of human error and ensures that you don't miss any critical payments that could disrupt your cash flow.

Reinvestment is another key element. A portion of your passive income should be consistently reinvested to fuel growth. Whether it's renovating a rental property, developing new digital products, or expanding your stock portfolio, reinvestment helps you scale your income streams. It's like planting seeds for future harvests.

Remember to keep an emergency fund. Unexpected expenses can and will happen. An emergency fund acts as a financial cushion, reducing the impact on your cash flow from sudden costs such as repairs or market downturns. It's wise to have at least three to six months' worth of expenses set aside in a liquid, easily accessible account.

Monitoring and evaluating your cash flow regularly is non-negotiable. Make it a habit to review your finances monthly. Assess which income streams are performing well and which ones aren't meeting expectations. This constant evaluation allows you to pivot and adjust strategies swiftly, maintaining a healthy cash flow.

Sometimes, despite our best planning, unforeseen challenges arise. That's when adjusting your cash flow strategy becomes necessary. If a particular income stream isn't performing, identify why and make the necessary adjustments. Maybe it's time to market your digital products differently, or perhaps a rental property's lease terms need re-negotiating. Being flexible and willing to adapt keeps your cash flow resilient.

Leverage debtor management for income streams involving clients or tenants. Ensure that all payments due to you are collected on time. Late payments can disrupt your cash flow significantly. Establish clear terms and make use of reminder systems to ensure you receive what's owed without delay.

Don't forget the importance of debt management. High-interest debts can erode your income quickly. If you're carrying any debt, prioritize paying off high-interest ones first. Reducing or eliminating debt frees up more of your cash flow for savings and reinvestment.

When scaling your income streams, balancing reinvestment with cash flow stability is crucial. It's tempting to throw all your earnings back into new ventures, but overextension can lead to cash shortages. Find a balance where you're both growing and maintaining a stable financial cushion.

Lastly, keep an eye on your tax obligations. Taxes can have a significant impact on your cash flow if not correctly managed. Consider consulting with a tax advisor to understand your liabilities and find legitimate ways to minimize your tax burden, such as through deductions and credits.

Achieving a steady cash flow in your passive income pursuits is all about balance and foresight. With the right strategies in place, you'll create a financial ecosystem that not only supports your current lifestyle but facilitates growth and expansion. Keep these principles in mind, and you'll find yourself well-prepared to manage your cash flow effectively, paving the way for lasting financial freedom.

Dealing with Failures and Setbacks

First things first, let's face it: there's no such thing as a perfectly smooth path to financial freedom. Dealing with failures and setbacks is an unavoidable aspect of the journey toward building multiple streams of passive income. However, these challenges shouldn't be seen as roadblocks, but rather as detours and learning opportunities on the road to long-term financial security.

One of the most common challenges you might face is the tendency to give up when things go wrong. It's crucial to remember that setbacks are not a reflection of your abilities or a sign that your goal is unattainable. Instead, they are feedback. Like a scientist testing a hypothesis, you need to view each failure as data that helps you refine your approach.

Consider the emotional roller coaster you might experience when a business venture doesn't yield expected results. It's easy to feel demoralized. However, dwelling on these negative emotions won't move you forward. Instead, you need to channel that energy into figuring out what went wrong and how you can avoid making the same mistakes in the future. Practicing resilience and developing a growth mindset are key here.

Let's talk about the financial aspect for a moment. A failed investment or an underperforming digital product can tighten your budget. This situation often tempts people to play it safe and forgo future risks. However, financial setbacks should be viewed through the lens of risk management. Diversifying your revenue streams early on can mitigate the impact of any single failure, enabling you to continue your journey without derailing your entire financial plan.

Failures and setbacks also often come with the harsh lesson of time management. It's easy to waste time stressing over what went wrong rather than moving forward. Making time for reflection is important, but it should be structured and purposeful. Set aside specific periods for analyzing your failures, followed by actionable steps to correct course, rather than letting it dominate your daily activities.

Another frequent hurdle is the social aspect of failure. You might feel embarrassed or worry about what others think of your setbacks. This is a natural human reaction, but it's important to remember that your journey is your own. Successful entrepreneurs have almost always faced doubts and criticism from others. Surround yourself with a supportive network that understands the ups and downs of building passive income streams.

Technology can also throw a wrench in your plans. Whether it's a platform change affecting your affiliate marketing income or a software glitch in your digital product, these setbacks are frustrating but solvable. Keeping abreast of technical developments and maintaining a backup plan can save you from spiraling into failure when technological changes occur.

Let's dive into regulatory and legal setbacks. These are often overlooked but can have a significant impact. Sudden changes in tax laws or compliance requirements can disrupt your income streams. Staying informed and perhaps even consulting with a financial advisor or legal expert can provide you with the guidance needed to navigate these choppy waters.

Market fluctuations are another external factor that can affect your passive income streams, particularly investments and real estate. While you can't control the market, you can control your reaction to it. By educating yourself on market trends and maintaining diversified investments, you'll be better positioned to handle these fluctuations without taking a significant hit to your income.

Another critical point is to consider the role of mentoring and coaching. Often, an element of failure can stem from not knowing what you don't know. Engaging with a mentor who has navigated similar challenges can offer invaluable insights and strategies. Their experiences can provide a roadmap for overcoming specific hurdles that you might be facing.

Additionally, setbacks offer the perfect opportunity to revisit and revise your strategy. Whether you need to pivot your approach or simply make slight adjustments, continuous improvement should be your mantra. Maybe your content needs to be more compelling, or perhaps your marketing strategies need an overhaul. Keep your goals flexible and adaptable to change.

Mindfulness and mental health shouldn't be ignored either. Stress and anxiety can cloud your judgment and hurt your decision-making abilities. Incorporating practices such as meditation, exercise, or even talking it out with a therapist can significantly improve your resilience and ability to cope with setbacks.

Incorporate lessons from your setbacks into future planning. A failed venture can teach you about market demand, customer needs, and even financial management. Documenting these lessons and integrating them into your strategy minimizes the chance of repeating past mistakes.

Failures and setbacks may ultimately serve as a crucible for your personal development. Mastery of passive income streams is as much about financial acumen as it is about personal growth. Embrace these challenges, not as obstacles, but as stepping stones. Often, the experience you gain and the resilience you build through navigating these setbacks will prove to be your most valuable assets.

In closing, failure isn't fatal. Dealing with setbacks can be tough, but using them as learning experiences will ultimately bring you closer to your goal of achieving financial freedom. Let each challenge sharpen your skills, deepen your knowledge, and strengthen your resolve. The journey will have bumps, but the destination makes it all worthwhile.

Ensuring Passive Income Sustainability

When you've built a variety of passive income streams, it can feel like you've finally hit that sweet spot of financial freedom. But the journey doesn't end there. Ensuring the sustainability of these income streams is equally critical. It's akin to nurturing a garden; without proper care, attention, and strategy, the fruits of your labor may wither. Let's dive into practical strategies and insights to keep your passive income thriving long-term.

Firstly, you need to understand that markets evolve, consumer behavior changes, and new technologies emerge. This dynamic nature means the passive income streams that are working well today may not be as robust tomorrow. Therefore, continuous learning and staying updated with market trends is essential. Never get too comfortable; always strive to innovate and adapt.

One way to achieve this is through diversification. Relying on a single source of passive income is like putting all your eggs in one basket. If that basket falls, you're left with nothing. Instead, spread your risk by investing in multiple income streams. For example, combine rental income with digital products and dividend investments. This way, if one stream underperforms, others can balance out the shortfall.

Another significant aspect is reinvesting a portion of your earnings back into your passive income ventures. This principle of compounding can exponentially grow your revenue over time. Whether it's upgrading your rental properties, expanding your digital product line, or buying more dividend-yielding stocks, reinvestment helps in sustaining and growing your income streams.

Automation is another powerful tool in ensuring passive income sustainability. The less hands-on you need to be, the more scalable and sustainable your operation becomes. Utilize technology to automate tasks such as marketing, customer service, and financial tracking. Tools like email marketing software, project management apps, and automated payment systems can save you time and minimize human error.

A comprehensive risk management strategy is also critical. Keeping a reserve fund can be a lifesaver during unforeseen circumstances like property vacancies, market crashes, or even health issues that might prevent you from being as involved as you'd like. Insurance products such as landlord insurance, product liability insurance, and health insurance provide additional layers of protection.

Don't underestimate the power of analytics. Regularly review your financial statements, website analytics, and market performance reports. These insights help you make informed decisions, identify declining income streams early, and take corrective actions. Keeping an eye on key performance indicators (KPIs) ensures that you're always aware of the health of your passive income portfolio.

Maintaining a network of advisors, mentors, and like-minded individuals is equally important. They can provide fresh perspectives, offer guidance, and even introduce you to new opportunities. Being part of a community or mastermind group dedicated to passive income can be incredibly beneficial for brainstorming and problem-solving.

Quality over quantity is another principle to live by. It's better to have a few well-managed and highly profitable income streams than dozens of poorly managed ones. Focus on optimizing and maximizing the efficiency of each stream. Streamline processes, cut unnecessary costs, and always look for ways to do things better.

Your mindset also plays a huge role in sustaining passive income. Cultivate an attitude of resilience and adaptability. Challenges are inevitable, but your ability to navigate through setbacks will determine your long-term success. Remember, every setback is an opportunity to learn and grow.

Moreover, legal and tax compliance can't be overlooked. Each passive income stream may come with its specific legal and tax obligations. Consult with a financial advisor or tax professional to ensure you're setting up the right business structures, taking advantage of legal tax breaks, and staying compliant with regulations.

Outsourcing tasks that don't require your direct involvement can free up your time for strategic thinking and planning. Whether it's hiring a property management company for your rentals or virtual assistants for digital tasks, leveraging other people's expertise can enhance the sustainability of your income streams.

Building a personal brand can create additional layers of passive income opportunities. If you're known as an expert in your field, you can generate income through speaking engagements, branded products, and endorsements. Your reputation can become a valuable asset that opens doors to various income avenues.

Lastly, but equally important, is ensuring your personal well-being. Sustainable income streams require a sustainable you. Burnout can derail even the best financial plans. Regularly take time for self-care, maintain a healthy work-life balance, and don't neglect your physical and mental health.

By putting these strategies into practice, you'll not only build but also sustain passive income streams that can provide financial security and independence for years to come. You're not just creating income; you're crafting a legacy of financial freedom.

Chapter 16:
Maintaining Balance and Well-being

As you journey towards financial freedom through multiple streams of passive income, maintaining balance and well-being is crucial. It's easy to get caught up in the hustle of setting up and managing various income sources, but without proper boundaries, burnout becomes inevitable. Prioritize self-care; allocate time for activities that rejuvenate you, whether that's exercising, spending time with loved ones, or simply unwinding with a good book. Continuous learning is another cornerstone of sustained success. Stay curious, embrace new knowledge, and adapt to ever-changing landscapes. By maintaining this balance, you not only ensure your ventures thrive but also enjoy the freedom and fulfillment that come with financial independence.

Setting Boundaries Between Work and Life

As you venture into building multiple streams of passive income, it can be incredibly easy to blur the lines between work and personal life. Setting boundaries between work and life isn't just a noble goal; it's a necessity for sustainable success and well-being. Without clear boundaries, you risk burnout, reduced productivity, and jeopardizing the quality time you could be spending with loved ones. Let's explore some practical ways to set and maintain these boundaries effectively.

First, understand that your home is not just a place for relaxation; it can also be a hotbed of distraction. Designating a specific workspace is crucial. Whether it's a dedicated room, a corner of your living room, or even a garage, having a clear physical separation helps signal your brain that it's time to work. This doesn't mean doing away with comfort, but it does mean setting up a space that fosters concentration and productivity. Once you're in that space, distractions should be minimized to maintain focus.

Your work hours should be as sacred as your personal time. Just as you wouldn't appreciate a friend calling you at 3 AM, your work hours should also have clear limits. Decide in advance what your typical work hours will be and stick to them. Communicate these boundaries with family and friends so they understand and respect your time. Utilizing tools like calendar apps can also help in maintaining structured work hours and preventing overflow into your personal time.

Technology can be both a blessing and a curse. While it enables the freedom to work from anywhere, it also creates an environment where you're always reachable. One effective strategy is to create a hard boundary by turning off email and work-related app notifications after a certain time of day. Set parameters for checking communication tools. For example, you might decide to check emails only twice a day rather than being constantly interrupted by notifications.

Developing a captivating morning routine that separates your day from night activities can also have a huge impact. This routine could involve meditation, exercise, or reading a book over your morning coffee. These activities help signal the beginning of a productive workday while also nurturing your well-being, setting you up for a day of focus and accomplishment.

It's equally important to have a clear end-of-day signal. This could be as simple as shutting down your computer, taking a walk, or spending time on a hobby. Engaging in an activity that marks the end of your workday can help you unwind and transition back to your personal life. By creating a ritual to signify the end of your workday, you help reinforce the work-life boundary.

Another effective method for maintaining work-life boundaries is time-blocking. Allocate specific blocks of time for tasks related to your various income streams and adhere to these schedules. This not only helps in maintaining focus but also ensures that you have time allocated for personal activities, family, and relaxation. Over time, this scheduling will become second nature, helping you strike a balance between productivity and personal time.

While setting boundaries, also remember to be kind to yourself. There will be days when work spills into personal time or vice versa. The key is to make these occurrences the exception rather than the rule. Being adaptable, while maintaining a firm framework, will help you weather these ebbs and flows without feeling guilty or overwhelmed.

A supportive network can make a world of difference. Surround yourself with people who understand and respect your boundaries, whether it's your family, friends, or professional network. Communicate openly about your needs and limitations, and don't be afraid to seek support or delegate tasks when necessary. This will not only help you maintain balance but also build stronger relationships based on mutual respect and understanding.

Living a balanced life also means making time for leisure and hobbies. Activities that bring you joy and relaxation are not optional. They are crucial for your mental and emotional well-being. Whether it's painting, hiking, or simply unwinding with a good movie, these activities replenish your energy and keep you motivated.

Incorporating spontaneous breaks throughout your day can have a significant positive impact. Short, frequent breaks help reset your focus and rejuvenate your mind. These breaks can be as simple as a five-minute walk, a coffee break, or even a few moments of quiet reflection. Over time, these small breaks help to sustain long-term productivity and well-being.

Mindfulness practices can also play a significant role in maintaining a balanced life. Techniques such as meditation, deep breathing exercises, or even journaling can help you stay grounded and focused. Mindfulness improves your ability to manage stress and maintain a clear distinction between work and personal life.

Lastly, don't underestimate the power of regular vacations or extended breaks. Stepping away from work entirely, even for a short period, can provide a fresh perspective and renewed energy. Plan these breaks in advance and ensure that your passive income streams are running smoothly without your constant oversight.

Incorporating these strategies into your routine can transform your work-life balance. Not only will you be more productive, but your overall happiness and satisfaction will also improve. Your journey towards financial freedom is not just about building wealth; it's about crafting a life that you enjoy and cherish.

Remember, setting boundaries isn't about restricting your freedom; it's about enhancing it. By clearly defining when and how you work, you create space for the personal joys and experiences that make life truly fulfilling. Start today, and take the steps toward achieving a balanced, fulfilling, and successful life.

The Importance of Self-Care

Embarking on the journey to financial freedom is exhilarating, but it can also be incredibly demanding. With countless strategies to implement and new skills to learn, it's easy to get caught up in the hustle and forget a crucial component of your success: self-care. Proper self-care isn't a luxury; it's an indispensable part of maintaining balance while pursuing passive income streams.

Let's face it, building multiple streams of passive income requires time, effort, and mental bandwidth. You're not just generating money;

you're crafting a new lifestyle that aligns with your financial goals. This commitment can often lead to burnout if not properly managed. That's why integrating self-care into your daily routine is paramount.

Self-care isn't just about pampering yourself with spa days or vacations, though those can be beneficial. It's also about the small, consistent practices that help you manage stress, maintain mental clarity, and stay physically healthy. It's about creating a balanced life that allows you to thrive, not just survive.

The link between physical health and financial success can't be overstated. Think about it: your energy levels, focus, and productivity significantly influence your ability to work on passive income projects. Regular exercise, a nutritious diet, and adequate sleep are foundational elements that can drastically improve your performance.

For instance, starting your day with a workout can be a game-changer. Physical activity boosts your mood, increases your energy, and enhances your focus. It's like setting a positive tone for the day that propels you to accomplish your goals more effectively. Small habits like taking breaks to stretch or walk can also make a big difference.

Proper self-care also encompasses mental and emotional well-being. Financial ventures can be stressful, especially when things don't go as planned. Practices like meditation, journaling, or even a few moments of deep breathing can help you manage stress and maintain a positive outlook. When your mind is clear and calm, you're better equipped to make smart decisions and tackle challenges head-on.

Another critical aspect of self-care is setting boundaries. In the pursuit of financial freedom, it can be tempting to work around the clock. However, putting limits on your work time and ensuring you allocate quality time for yourself and your loved ones is crucial. Not only does this prevent burnout, but it also enriches your personal life, which indirectly enhances your professional endeavors.

In addition, self-care encourages ongoing self-improvement and learning. Whether it's reading books, taking courses, or attending workshops, constantly feeding your mind with new knowledge and varying perspectives can ignite creativity and innovation in your passive income strategies. Self-care facilitates this continuous growth by keeping you energized and motivated.

Let's not overlook the social aspects of self-care. Financial independence can sometimes be a lonely journey. Having a supportive community or a network of like-minded individuals can provide emotional support, motivation, and new ideas. Taking time to nurture these relationships can enrich your journey and keep you grounded.

Moreover, self-care empowers you to enjoy the fruits of your labor. Achieving financial freedom shouldn't come at the cost of your happiness and well-being. Take time to celebrate your successes, no matter how small. Reward yourself for hitting milestones, and you'll find that these positive reinforcements keep you energized and focused on your long-term goals.

It's important to remember that self-care isn't one-size-fits-all. What works for someone else might not work for you. The key is to find practices that resonate with you and incorporate them into your daily routine. Self-care should be personalized to meet your specific needs and preferences.

In summary, the importance of self-care in your quest for financial freedom cannot be overstated. It's not just an add-on; it's a necessity. By prioritizing your physical, mental, and emotional well-being, you're not just enhancing your quality of life; you're also setting yourself up for sustainable success. So, take that first step towards integrating self-care into your routine and watch how it transforms your journey to financial freedom.

Remember, the goal isn't just to build passive income streams; it's to create a life of balance, well-being, and fulfillment. Proper self-care is the bridge to achieving this holistic success. Let it be the anchor that keeps you steady as you navigate the exciting, and sometimes turbulent, waters of financial independence.

Self-care is more than a routine; it's a proactive strategy to ensure you not only reach your financial goals but also enjoy the journey along the way. Investing in yourself is the best investment you can make, because a healthier, happier you is the ultimate foundation for a prosperous and balanced life.

Embracing Continuous Learning

When it comes to achieving long-term financial freedom through passive income, embracing continuous learning isn't just an option; it's a necessity. Staying current with new trends, tools, and strategies can make the difference between just getting by and truly thriving. Think of continuous learning as your secret weapon, an ongoing investment in yourself that pays dividends far greater than any stock or rental property could.

In the constantly evolving landscape of passive income, what worked yesterday might not work tomorrow. Digital marketing algorithms change, market trends shift, and new technologies emerge. To keep up, you need to be a lifelong student. The mindset of continuous learning allows you to remain adaptable, an indispensable quality in the dynamic world of passive income streams.

First off, make learning a daily habit. Set aside a specific time each day dedicated solely to education. Whether it's reading industry news, taking online courses, or listening to podcasts, make this a non-negotiable part of your routine. You're already managing multiple streams of passive income; imagine how much more efficient and profitable you could be with just a bit more knowledge under your belt.

Then, look for mentors and peer groups. Surround yourself with people who are as committed to learning and growth as you are. Whether through online forums, mastermind groups, or local meetups, networking with like-minded individuals can offer you fresh perspectives and keep your motivation high. Just the act of discussing ideas or challenges with others can provide invaluable insights that you might not have considered on your own.

Consider diversifying your learning sources. Don't get all your information from just books or videos. Attend webinars, workshops, and live events. Participate in online forums and interact with experts in your field. Leverage different kinds of media—videos, articles, podcasts, and interactive courses. Each medium has its unique set of advantages and can help solidify your understanding from multiple angles.

Being well-versed in multiple subjects related to passive income can set you apart. For instance, understanding the basics of coding can give you an edge when developing digital products or optimizing an e-commerce store. Similarly, a grasp of financial markets and investment principles can make your portfolio more resilient. The more you know, the more tools you have at your disposal to build and manage a diversified income stream.

Remember, the goal isn't to become an expert overnight but to make steady progress. Incremental gains accumulated over time can lead to significant advancements in your knowledge and decision-making capabilities. Commit to just one hour of learning each day, and you'll find that you've logged hundreds of hours of valuable education by the year's end.

Feedback is another critical component of continuous learning. Don't shy away from constructive criticism. Whether it comes from customer reviews, analytics data, or peer assessments, use this feedback to improve and pivot where necessary. The most successful passive income earners are those who are not afraid to tweak their strategies based on real-world feedback.

Consider the potential setbacks not as failures but as learning opportunities. Every obstacle you encounter is a chance to gain valuable lessons that you can apply moving forward. The key is not to avoid mistakes but to learn from them quickly and efficiently. When you adopt this mindset, you transform challenges into stepping stones toward greater success.

Reading is powerful, but practical application solidifies learning. Try to implement what you learn as soon as you learn it. For example, if you pick up a new SEO technique, apply it to your website right away. Immediate application helps embed the knowledge into your working memory, making it more likely that you'll remember and skillfully use it in the future.

Staying updated on market conditions and consumer behaviors is also crucial. This can include subscribing to newsletters in your niche, regularly checking analytics, and staying active on social media to understand current trends. You don't have to act on every piece of information you come across, but being informed allows you to make educated decisions.

Continuous learning is also about passing on the knowledge. Teaching others what you've learned can significantly enhance your own understanding. Create content, write blog posts, host webinars, or simply mentor someone who is just starting out. The act of explaining complex topics forces you to organize your thoughts and deepen your comprehension.

Your learning journey doesn't end when you achieve a certain level of success. The most successful people in any industry are those who never stop learning. They stay curious, keep asking questions, and always look for ways to innovate and improve. Make learning a cornerstone of your life, and you'll continuously find new opportunities for growth and profit.

Finally, cultivate a growth mindset. Believe that your abilities and intelligence can be developed over time. This mindset encourages you to see challenges as opportunities and fosters a love for learning. People with a growth mindset are more resilient and adaptable, qualities that are incredibly valuable in the passive income arena.

In conclusion, embracing continuous learning equips you with the knowledge and skills needed to maneuver through the ever-changing landscape of passive income. By being persistent, staying curious, and committing to your ongoing education, you ensure that your passive income streams are not just sustainable, but also scalable. The investment you make in your own learning pays off in ways you might not even imagine.

Chapter 17:
The Future of Passive Income

The landscape of passive income is rapidly evolving, and staying ahead of the curve means recognizing and capitalizing on emerging trends and opportunities. The digital age continues to unlock new avenues for income generation, from blockchain investments to AI-driven revenue models. To thrive in the future, adaptability and resilience will be key—embracing new technologies, pivoting strategies when necessary, and continually learning. Moreover, creating passive income streams that don't just serve us, but also leave a lasting legacy for future generations, can transform financial freedom into something truly enduring. Now is the time to plant the seeds for tomorrow's harvest, utilizing every tool and innovation at our disposal to build a sustainable, prosperous future.

Emerging Trends and Opportunities

As we move further into the digital age, the landscape of passive income continues to evolve, offering new opportunities that were unimaginable just a few years ago. With technology advancing at an unprecedented rate, it's crucial to stay ahead of the curve and leverage these emerging trends to build a robust passive income portfolio.

One of the most exciting trends we are seeing is the rise of blockchain and cryptocurrency. Cryptocurrencies like Bitcoin and Ethereum have not only opened new avenues for investment but also introduced concepts such as staking and yield farming. These methods allow you to earn passive income by locking up your crypto assets in a network to support operations like transaction validation. The rewards, often in the form of additional tokens or coins, present a new form of generating passive income that can be incredibly lucrative.

Another groundbreaking development is the proliferation of decentralized finance, or DeFi. DeFi platforms function without traditional banks and offer services like lending, borrowing, and earning interest on crypto assets. DeFi has democratized finance, enabling anyone with an internet connection to participate. These platforms often provide higher returns on investments compared to traditional banks, making them an attractive option for passive income generation.

Speaking of technology, artificial intelligence (AI) and machine learning are playing a transformative role in investment and business strategies. AI algorithms can now be employed to automate trading, optimizing profit margins, and mitigating risks. Automated trading bots can execute trades at lightning speed, ensuring that your investments are always working for you, even while you sleep. This puts passive income on autopilot, requiring minimal intervention and offering peace of mind.

Moreover, the gig economy is extending its influence into passive income avenues. Take, for instance, the rise of fractional ownership models. Platforms now allow you to own a fraction of high-value assets like real estate, luxury vehicles, and even fine art. These investments generate income through rentals or sales, and the fractional ownership model lowers the entry barrier, enabling more people to participate in wealth-building opportunities.

The increasing acceptance of remote work also opens up the potential for geo-arbitrage. Living in a low-cost country while earning income from high-cost countries can significantly amplify your savings and investments. This strategy stretches your dollar further, paving the way for a higher rate of return and quicker financial independence.

Fostering a community-driven approach to income generation, social commerce and the sharing economy are generating new revenue streams. Platforms like Etsy and Poshmark enable individuals to monetize their hobbies and crafts, transforming passions into profitable ventures. Likewise, the peer-to-peer rental market, exemplified by websites like Turo for car rentals, provides opportunities to earn passive income by making personal assets available for rent.

Online education is a booming sector where knowledge transforms into wealth. Creating and selling online courses or offering subscription-based educational content can develop into a steady income stream. As more people seek to upskill and reskill, the demand for online learning platforms has never been higher. If you have expertise in a particular field, this is a ripe opportunity to tap into a global audience.

Content creation still stands as a prominent avenue, but it's constantly evolving. Gone are the days when blogging was the sole method of generating passive income through content. Today, podcasting and YouTube channels provide equally lucrative opportunities. Sponsorships, ad revenues, and affiliate marketing deals are just some of the ways through which content creators can earn substantial passive income.

Subscription models offer another innovative way to generate recurring passive income. Platforms like Substack allow you to charge readers a monthly fee for access to in-depth articles or exclusive content. This model not only ensures a consistent income stream but also nurtures a dedicated community and fosters deeper engagement.

With the advent of virtual reality (VR) and augmented reality (AR), new experiences are being crafted in digital domains. Imagine owning digital real estate within a VR platform and renting it out for virtual events, tours, or experiences. The demand for immersive experiences is growing, and early adopters in this space stand to benefit significantly.

Non-fungible tokens (NFTs) are revolutionizing the art and entertainment industries by providing a new way to buy, sell, and trade digital assets. Artists, musicians, and even gamers are discovering ways to generate passive income through royalties and resale rights embedded in NFTs.

Subscription box services are another niche but potent way to rake in passive income. Curating a mix of products tailored to specific interests and delivering them to subscribers on a monthly basis can build a dedicated customer base. The beauty of this model is its scalability and the relatively low overhead costs involved.

In the eco-conscious marketplace, sustainable and ethical investments are gaining traction. Green bonds, renewable energy projects, and sustainable agriculture offer avenues for passive income while contributing positively to the environment. Investing in these responsible ventures not only provides financial returns but also aligns with a growing societal emphasis on sustainability.

Lastly, think about the power of data. Data is the new oil, and owning or operating a data platform can open avenues for passive income through subscriptions, data sales, or targeted advertising. Whether through creating data products or facilitating data services, the opportunities in this area are vast and constantly expanding.

To make the most of these emerging trends, continuous learning and adaptability are crucial. The world of passive income is dynamic, and staying ahead requires an open mind and a willingness to embrace new opportunities as they arise.

Staying Adaptable and Resilient

As we journey into the future of passive income, one thing you'll come to realize is the absolute necessity of staying adaptable and resilient. The landscape of financial opportunities is constantly shifting, influenced by technological advances, market trends, and societal changes. To ensure your passive income streams don't dry up, being able to pivot and bounce back from setbacks is crucial.

Start by embracing the mindset that change is inevitable. Whether it's a new social media platform altering how affiliate marketing is done or a sudden dip in the stock market, disruptions will occur. By anticipating change rather than resisting it, you'll set yourself up for long-term sustainability. It's easy to feel comfortable when things are going well, but remember, it's the unexpected that often tests our resolve.

Next, your strategy should always include a component of learning and skill acquisition. The digital age offers a myriad of online courses, webinars, and tutorials on virtually any subject you can think of. Make it a habit to devote time regularly to upgrading your skills. Whether it's learning about new investment opportunities or advancements in digital marketing tactics, continuous learning will keep you ahead of the game.

Engage in community or networking events. These could be industry-specific seminars, online webinars, or even local meetups. The aim is to build and maintain a network of like-minded individuals who can provide support, share knowledge, and offer fresh perspectives. You'll be surprised how often an offhand comment or a casual conversation can spark an idea that transforms your passive income strategy.

Don't be afraid to diversify your income streams. We've covered various ways to generate passive income in this book, from rental properties to digital products and stock market dividends. Relying on a single stream can put you at risk. By diversifying, you spread that risk around, increasing your chances of maintaining steady income even if one source falters.

Analyzing and reassessing your portfolio frequently is another important part of staying adaptable. What worked last year may not work this year due to market fluctuations or changes in consumer behavior. Have regular check-ins with your financial advisor if you have one, or spend time evaluating your investments yourself. Staying informed will help you make timely adjustments and leverage new opportunities.

Embrace technology. Automation tools, AI-driven analytics, and other emerging technologies can provide new ways to manage and grow your passive income streams efficiently. Whether it's automating your email marketing campaigns or using software to manage your rental properties, technology offers solutions that not only save time but can also boost your income.

Emotional resilience is equally important as strategic adaptability. The journey to financial freedom isn't always a smooth one. You will face challenges and setbacks. What will matter most is how you respond to these obstacles. Cultivating a positive attitude and resilience will help you bounce back from failures and embrace new opportunities with vigor.

Drill down into the specifics of stress management techniques which resonate with you. Whether it's meditation, exercise, or enjoying a hobby, knowing how to de-stress will keep you mentally prepared for the ups and downs that come with managing multiple income streams.

Setbacks are part of the journey, and each failure presents a learning opportunity. Reflect on what went wrong, analyze your mistakes, and use those lessons to refine your strategies. A setback might expose a weakness in your approach or open up avenues you hadn't considered before.

Building a financial cushion is another critical aspect of staying resilient. Having an emergency fund separate from your investment capital ensures you can handle unexpected expenses without disrupting your income streams. This financial safety net provides peace of mind and keeps you focused on growth rather than survival.

Flexibility also means being open to feedback. Whether it's customer reviews on your digital products or advice from a mentor, take feedback seriously. Constructive criticism can offer valuable insights that help you improve and adapt your offerings, keeping you competitive in the market.

Finally, leverage the power of goal setting to keep your focus intact. Establish short-term and long-term goals, and regularly review and adjust them as needed. This provides direction and a sense of purpose, ensuring you remain committed to your journey even when challenges arise.

To sum up, staying adaptable and resilient is not a one-time effort but an ongoing process. It's about cultivating a mindset that's open to change, continuously learning, diversifying your income sources, and maintaining emotional and financial resilience. These qualities will not just help you survive the future of passive income, but thrive in it, setting you firmly on the path to financial freedom.

Creating a Legacy

When we talk about creating a legacy, we're not just looking at what kind of wealth or assets you can leave behind. We're looking at the positive impact your success can have on future generations, your community, and possibly even the world. A legacy in the context of passive income is about building something sustainable and meaningful that extends beyond your own life.

First, let's think about the financial security aspect. Passive income streams, once established, have the potential to continue generating income with minimal effort from your end. This means that you can secure not just your future, but also provide financial stability for your family. Imagine a scenario where your children are debt-free through college because of the investments you've made. That's the profound impact of building a legacy.

Beyond financial security, consider the potential for educational opportunities. The lessons you learn on this journey—whether it's mastering real estate or honing digital product creation—are incredibly valuable. Passing down this knowledge can empower the next generation to harness their own income streams without becoming slaves to the traditional 9-to-5 grind. If you document your strategies and sharing your learning experiences, you're offering a roadmap for others to follow.

It's also about inspiring others. When you become successful in generating passive income, you serve as a living example of what's possible. Others may look at your journey and feel motivated to take their own path towards financial freedom. Sometimes, the best legacy you can leave is simply the inspiration and belief that it's achievable.

We should mention the societal impact here too. Financial independence often brings with it the time and resources to contribute positively to society. You could support local businesses, contribute to charitable causes, or even start initiatives that address social issues. The ripple effect of your financial success could extend well beyond your immediate circle.

Legacy is also intertwined with innovation. Many successful passive income ventures are built on groundbreaking ideas. Perhaps your digital products introduce new learning methods, or your investment tactics become case studies for future entrepreneurs. These innovations can pave the way for new opportunities and advancements within various fields.

Moreover, as you create robust passive income streams, you're also creating assets that can be inherited. This not only includes financial assets but intellectual properties like books, digital courses, and software. These assets can continue to generate income long after you've stepped back, providing lasting benefits to your heirs.

Emphatically, think about the personal legacy. What sort of values do you want to pass on? Being involved in passive income generation often requires a mindset of resilience, patience, and strategic thinking. By involving younger generations in your endeavors, you can instill these valuable traits, helping them develop a strong work ethic and an entrepreneurial mindset.

To bring this into focus, let's consider the concept of financial literacy. A significant part of your legacy could be educational, teaching your children and even community about managing money effectively. By fostering an understanding of investments, savings, and the importance of financial independence, you are contributing to a more financially aware society.

By diversifying your passive income streams, you also teach the importance of not putting all eggs in one basket. This avoids dependence on a single income source, which is a valuable lesson in risk management. This approach can be crucial during economic downturns or unexpected life events.

In the digital age, leaving a legacy includes having a significant online presence. Consider content creation: blogs, podcasts, or

YouTube channels that document your journey and advice. These platforms can outlive us and continue to provide value to others. It's a modern twist on the classic idea of writing a book or teaching a course.

Let's not forget about succession planning. As you scale your passive income ventures, planning for a smooth transition is key. Whether it's mentoring someone to take over your real estate investments or setting up a trust for your digital products, ensuring your assets are well-managed after you're gone is crucial to sustaining your legacy.

Creating a legacy also allows you to leave behind not just wealth, but a lasting mark of your core values and the impact you aimed to have. It's about more than just money; it's about the lessons, values, and inspiration you impart to your family and community.

Legacy-building isn't something that happens automatically; it requires forethought and planning. It's the culmination of a series of purposeful decisions aimed at creating something of lasting value. And once you've successfully created diverse streams of passive income, you'll find you have the freedom and peace of mind to focus on this larger goal.

So as you navigate through the intricate world of passive income, remember: you're not just working for financial freedom. You're crafting something that can give back to your family, community, and future generations. That's the true essence of creating a legacy.

Chapter 18:
Real-Life Success Stories

When chasing the dream of financial freedom through passive income, real-life success stories can serve as powerful motivators. Take, for instance, Sarah, who transitioned from a stressed-out 9-to-5 job to managing a portfolio of rental properties that eventually allowed her to travel the world while her income kept flowing. Then there's Mike, who took a leap of faith into the world of digital products by launching an online course that now earns him a six-figure income annually. These stories aren't just outliers; they demonstrate that with consistent effort, proper planning, and unwavering determination, ordinary individuals can achieve extraordinary results. It's not about overnight success or giving up when challenges arise; it's about learning from those who've been there, navigating the ups and downs, and ultimately creating a sustainable passive income stream that secures your financial future.

From Side Hustle to Full-Time Passive Income

Turning a simple side hustle into a full-time passive income stream isn't just a dream. It's a reality for many who've leveraged the right strategies at the right time. Take, for instance, Sarah, a graphic designer from Austin, Texas. She started by selling custom illustrations on a popular online marketplace. Initially, it was a way to make some extra cash on weekends. Little did she know, this side gig would eventually replace her 9-to-5 job.

Sarah's journey began modestly. She took on small projects while maintaining her day job. Over time, she built a portfolio and generated positive reviews. Her secret? Consistency and a keen eye for trends. She noticed a growing demand for personalized wedding invitations, so she shifted her focus. By specializing, Sarah could charge a premium, and her customer base grew rapidly.

Eventually, she decided to create printable templates, a passive income model. Rather than custom orders, customers could buy and download these templates directly, freeing Sarah to focus on creating more products. Her earnings soared, and she was soon making more from her side hustle than her day job. Leaving her 9-to-5 was a calculated risk she was finally ready to take.

Then there's Miguel, a software developer turned entrepreneur. Miguel started with affiliate marketing. In his spare time, he reviewed tech gadgets on a blog he monetized through affiliate links. Initially, the blog had modest traffic, but Miguel was diligent about SEO and content quality. He knew the key was to build trust with his audience.

Through trial and error, Miguel learned what resonated with his readers. Detailed, unbiased reviews with high-quality images and honest pros and cons provided value. Over time, his blog's traffic increased, and so did his affiliate commissions. Seeing the potential, Miguel began treating his blog as a business.

He automated parts of the process, like link insertion and email marketing, to save time. He outsourced content creation to focus on strategy and growth. His affiliate income became substantial enough to outweigh his developer's salary, allowing him to explore other passive income ventures like digital products and online courses.

Consider also Jane and Rafael, a couple who started with real estate investments. They purchased their first rental property with the goal of supplementing their income. For a while, it was a juggling act. They managed tenants and maintenance issues while continuing their day jobs. But they made it work by setting clear roles and responsibilities.

Their "aha" moment came when they realized they could scale this model. By refinancing their first property, they bought a second one and then a third. They optimized their time by hiring a property management company, freeing up their hours while still reaping rental income. Today, Jane and Rafael enjoy monthly passive income that far exceeds their previous combined salaries.

What do all these stories have in common? A key factor: leveraging automation and outsourcing. Whether it's printable digital products, content creation, or property management, automation reduces the active involvement needed. Concurrently, outsourcing takes care of specialized tasks, allowing one to focus on scaling.

Moreover, they've all overcome their fear of stepping away from a stable paycheck. Sarah and Miguel had to validate their business models before leaving their jobs. Jane and Rafael used strategically financed growth to minimize risk. The transition is never entirely smooth, but calculated steps make it feasible.

Also pivotal is their focus on diversification. None of these individuals relied solely on one income source. Sarah branched out into multiple marketplaces and products. Miguel diversified from affiliate marketing to digital courses. Jane and Rafael diversified their rental property types and locations.

Patience is another common thread. The shift from side hustle to full-time passive income doesn't happen overnight. It requires consistent effort, ongoing learning, and occasional reinvention. These success stories highlight that setbacks will occur, but resilience and adaptability are crucial for long-term success.

Another noteworthy element is continuous improvement. All these individuals kept evolving. Sarah took courses on digital marketing. Miguel stayed updated on SEO trends and affiliate programs. Jane and Rafael attended real estate seminars. Improvement is an ongoing process, essential for staying ahead of the curve.

Trust the process, but also trust yourself. It's easy to get overwhelmed by the initial challenges and uncertainties. Yet, these narratives illustrate the importance of believing in your capabilities. Small, consistent actions lead to monumental changes in the long run.

These success stories aren't just about financial freedom. They highlight the empowerment and confidence gained along the journey. Each step taken towards passive income is a step away from dependency on the 9-to-5 grind, leading to a life with more choices and less stress.

Real-life transformations from side hustles to full-time passive income are happening every day. They're not the results of overnight successes or get-rich-quick schemes. They are the outcomes of strategic moves, calculated risks, and unwavering persistence. If they can do it, so can you. Your journey might be unique, but the principles and strategies are universal.

Overcoming Adversity

When it comes to achieving financial freedom through passive income, adversity is practically a given. But what sets successful individuals apart isn't whether they face challenges—it's how they handle them. Real-life stories of those who've walked this path are invaluable. They offer not just inspiration, but practical lessons in resilience and innovation.

One such story is that of Linda, a single mother who lost her job during a widespread corporate downsizing. With no immediate job prospects and a child to support, she turned to her passion for knitting. Linda began selling handmade scarves on Etsy. Sales were slow initially, but she stayed committed, learning everything she could about digital marketing and customer engagement. Over time, her Etsy shop grew into a robust online business, enabling her to transition from just making ends meet to thriving off passive income through digital knitting patterns.

Linda's journey wasn't straightforward. Along the way, she faced nights filled with self-doubt and days when sales were nonexistent. Yet she persevered, armed with a mindset that each failure was a lesson rather than a setback. It's this mindset shift—from viewing obstacles as insurmountable walls to seeing them as opportunities for growth—that plays a crucial role in overcoming adversity.

Take John, a young real estate investor who thought he had it all figured out. He acquired a few rental properties and was poised for success. Then, a severe economic downturn hit, and tenants started defaulting on rent. John found himself under tremendous financial strain. Instead of surrendering to despair, he decided to get creative. John moved some of his properties to short-term rentals through Airbnb, tapping into a different market segment. This pivot saved his business and eventually led to higher returns than he had initially projected.

John's story highlights another critical aspect of overcoming adversity: adaptability. The world of passive income isn't static; it demands constant reevaluation and flexibility. By being willing to adapt his strategy to the changing market conditions, John was able to not just survive but ultimately thrive.

Patricia's experience adds another layer to this tapestry of resilience. She built a blog that generated significant ad revenue, only to have a major algorithm change by a search engine slash her traffic and income overnight. Rather than throwing in the towel, Patricia took this as a sign to diversify. She added affiliate marketing, created and sold digital courses, and even started a podcast. Diversifying her income streams meant that no single algorithm change could jeopardize her financial stability again.

In Patricia's case, the key lesson is diversification. Relying on a single source of passive income can be risky. By spreading out her income streams, Patricia built a more stable and resilient financial foundation. Challenges forced her to become more innovative and fortified her against future uncertainties.

Similarly, Oscar faced his share of trials in the tech world. An app he developed and poured his savings into was met with lukewarm reception. Low downloads and tepid reviews seemed like the end of his dream. However, Oscar pivoted by gathering extensive user feedback and redeveloped the app based on real user needs and preferences. This revamp turned his struggling project into a profitable venture, bringing in steady revenue month after month.

Oscar's comeback underscores the significance of customer feedback. Sometimes adversity comes in the form of market rejection, and the best way to bounce back is by closely listening to what potential consumers really want. His ability to adapt his product based on feedback was instrumental in making his app successful.

Julie's journey from a hectic 9-to-5 to living off passive income demonstrates the power of patience. She initially faced many hurdles, from ineffective marketing strategies to time management issues. Julie dedicated herself to learning and iterating her approach. With consistent effort over several years, she established multiple streams of income, ranging from online courses to dividends from investments. Julie's story emphasizes that success often doesn't come quickly, but with patience and persistent effort, adversities can be overcome.

Another noteworthy story is Carlos, a retiree who invested in stocks to build a passive income portfolio. The stock market's volatility was a significant challenge, leading to periods of substantial financial stress. Carlos educated himself about market behaviors, dividends, and investment diversification. Over time, his disciplined approach paid off. His dividend portfolio now generates a steady stream of passive income, allowing him to enjoy his retirement without financial worries.

Carlos's story teaches us about the importance of financial literacy. Understanding the market and making informed decisions can turn a seemingly adverse situation into a profitable endeavor. His steadfast commitment to learning and applying that knowledge was crucial in overcoming financial ups and downs.

Even younger enthusiasts like Emma, who turned her love for fitness into a thriving online business, faced setbacks. Her initial fitness videos received little traction. But Emma didn't give up; she improved her content quality, posted consistently, and engaged actively with her audience on social media. Today, her fitness empire generates significant income through ads, sponsorships, and an exclusive membership website.

Emma's persistence and willingness to engage with her audience exemplify how building a solid community can help overcome adversity in the digital content world. Her journey shows that developing a loyal following can translate into various passive income opportunities.

The road to passive income is rarely smooth, but these stories illustrate that overcoming adversity is part and parcel of the journey. Each challenge faced by these individuals provided valuable lessons that propelled them forward. They adapted, learned, diversified, and, most importantly, didn't give up.

So, when adversity knocks, remember these real-life success stories. Understand that setbacks are stepping stones, not roadblocks. Every problem encountered is an opportunity to innovate, adapt, and grow.

With this mindset, no obstacle is insurmountable on your path to financial freedom.

Lessons Learned and Key Takeaways

After diving into real-life success stories of individuals who have managed to escape the nine-to-five grind and build multiple streams of passive income, several key lessons and takeaways emerge. Let's explore these insights, which can serve as a guide for anyone aiming to achieve financial freedom.

1. Start Small but Think Big

One common theme among the success stories is that most people started with small, manageable projects. Whether it was a single rental property or a modest e-commerce store, the initial steps were often small. However, they didn't remain small-minded. They always had a bigger vision and strategically worked towards it.

2. Diversification is Crucial

Another significant lesson is the importance of diversifying income streams. Relying on a single source of income, even if it's passive, can be risky. Successful individuals often spread their efforts across multiple channels—real estate, investing, digital products, and more—ensuring stability even if one stream falters.

3. Perseverance Pays Off

The journey to financial freedom is rarely a straight line. Most real-life success stories included bumps along the road, whether it was a failed business venture or an investment that didn't pan out. The key takeaway here is perseverance. Sticking to the plan, learning from failures, and continuing to push forward proves to be a winning strategy.

4. Continuous Learning and Adaptation

Markets and opportunities are always evolving. The most successful people are those who continually educate themselves and adapt their strategies accordingly. This might mean taking a course on a new type of digital marketing or learning about emerging investment opportunities. Lifelong learning is a critical component of long-term success.

5. Building a Strong Network

Relationships matter a lot. Many stories highlighted how mentors, peers, and professional networks played an instrumental role in their journey. Networking opens doors to opportunities, resources, and the collective wisdom of those who have walked similar paths.

6. Leveraging Technology

In today's age, technology provides unprecedented leverage. From automated email sequences to dropshipping platforms, leveraging technology was a recurring theme among those who succeeded. They utilized tools to automate tasks, optimize processes, and scale their businesses efficiently.

7. Importance of a Solid Foundation

Whether it's financial literacy, understanding the basics of investing, or grasping the intricacies of digital marketing, having a strong foundational knowledge is essential. Most successful stories started with the individual investing time in learning the fundamentals before diving into execution.

8. Emotional Resilience

The emotional element can't be overstated. Financial ups and downs can be stressful, and maintaining psychological resilience is critical. Many success stories included aspects of mental health strategies, such as mindfulness or regular exercise, to stay balanced and focused.

9. Setting Clear Goals

Setting specific, measurable, achievable, relevant, and time-bound (SMART) goals was a consistent practice. Clear goals not only provide direction but also make it easier to track progress and adapt strategies as needed.

10. Taking Calculated Risks

Risk is inherent in any entrepreneurial journey, but the key is to take calculated risks. Successful individuals did thorough research, weighed the pros and cons, and made informed decisions rather than jumping in blindly.

11. The Power of Reinvesting

Instead of spending all their profits, many successful individuals reinvested a significant portion back into their income streams. This practice of reinvesting accelerated growth and helped build more substantial, sustainable passive income.

12. Strategic Outsourcing

As their ventures grew, outsourcing became a necessity. Delegating tasks that were not core to their expertise allowed them to focus on strategic growth. This was crucial for scaling operations without getting bogged down by day-to-day tasks.

13. Importance of Legal and Financial Structures

Proper legal and financial setups provided a safety net and facilitated smoother operations. Whether it was forming an LLC or understanding tax implications, having the right structures in place made a big difference.

14. Maintaining Work-Life Balance

Maintaining a balance between work and personal life was cited as essential for long-term sustainability. Those who managed to keep a healthy balance avoided burnout and enjoyed the journey towards financial freedom more.

15. Paying It Forward

Finally, a notable aspect was giving back. Many successful individuals felt a sense of duty to help others on similar journeys. Whether through mentorship, sharing knowledge, or philanthropy, giving back added a layer of fulfillment and meaning to their financial success.

These insights provide a roadmap for anyone looking to transition from a traditional job to achieving financial independence through passive income. Each lesson, grounded in real-life experiences, offers actionable advice and inspiration to chart your own path to financial freedom.

Your Path to Financial Freedom

As you reach the final chapter of this journey, it's time to reflect on everything you've learned and set your sights on the road ahead. You've been equipped with a wealth of knowledge, from understanding various types of passive income to grasping the crucial mindset needed for success. This isn't just about adding more dollars to your bank account; it's about designing a life that allows you to live on your terms, free from the constant grind of a 9-to-5 job.

The essence of financial freedom is choice. Having multiple streams of passive income gives you the freedom to make decisions based on your aspirations rather than financial constraints. Whether it's spending more time with family, exploring new hobbies, or traveling the world, your options expand significantly. This flexibility is the ultimate goal, and it's entirely within your reach if you commit to the strategies and principles laid out in this book.

Creating passive income streams is not the same as chasing quick riches. It's a deliberate, calculated process that requires time, effort, and a significant shift in mindset. If you remember, we discussed debunking myths and facing the reality of passive income. You know now that it's about consistency and the willingness to persevere through the initial stages where results may seem minimal.

Your journey to financial freedom begins with an essential shift—from focusing on active earnings to building passive wealth. This transition is foundational, as it aligns your actions with long-term goals rather than short-term gains. You've been encouraged to cultivate patience and persistence, both of which are crucial in overcoming the fear and doubt that often accompany new ventures.

Setting clear, attainable goals is another cornerstone of this journey. Your objectives will be your guiding star, helping you navigate through the complexities of financial planning and investment. Understanding where you currently stand financially allows you to set realistic milestones, track your progress, and make informed decisions.

Financial literacy is indispensable. As you delve into areas such as real estate, digital products, and stock investments, a solid foundation in financial knowledge will empower you to make smarter choices. Without this, even the most lucrative opportunities can become overwhelming and risky.

Real estate remains one of the most reliable sources of passive income, whether through rental properties, REITs, or short-term rentals. As you've learned, each approach has its nuances, but all offer compelling returns if managed wisely. Your ability to discern market conditions and property value will significantly impact your success in this domain.

On the digital front, the creation and marketing of products like eBooks, online courses, and mobile applications represent another lucrative avenue. Identifying your niche and crafting content that resonates with your audience can lead to sustainable income streams. Remember, the internet offers unparalleled scalability, allowing your efforts to reach a global audience.

Stock market investments, particularly dividends and ETFs, are other crucial elements of a diversified passive income portfolio. Understanding the mechanisms of these financial instruments and building a balanced portfolio can contribute immensely to your financial security.

Affiliate marketing, dropshipping, and e-commerce are more advanced strategies that hinge on your ability to leverage the power of the internet. Building and monetizing websites, creating compelling content, and optimizing your operations through automation will all play significant roles in your success.

Don't overlook the power of blogging and social media. Beyond being mere platforms for expression, they can be powerful income generators when approached with a strategic mindset. By effectively utilizing SEO, crafting engaging content, and exploring various monetization methods, you can create significant income streams.

Email marketing—often underrated—can be a goldmine for generating passive income. Building a substantial email list, creating valuable lead magnets, and deploying automated campaigns can offer sustained revenue with minimal ongoing effort.

As you scale and optimize these streams, diversification becomes paramount. It's not just about having multiple sources but ensuring they are robust and resilient against market fluctuations. Continuous reinvestment and automation will free up your time and energy for new ventures.

Your path will inevitably include legal and regulatory considerations. Setting up the right business structures, understanding tax implications, and protecting your assets should be integral parts of your strategy. These measures will safeguard your income and ensure long-term sustainability.

Challenges will arise—it's part of the journey. Managing cash flow, dealing with setbacks, and ensuring the sustainability of your income streams will test your resolve. However, each challenge is an opportunity to grow and refine your approach.

Maintaining balance is indispensable. Setting boundaries, prioritizing self-care, and embracing continuous learning will help you stay grounded and focused. Remember, financial freedom is not just about wealth but also about well-being and personal fulfillment.

Finally, look towards the future with optimism. Stay adaptable, keep an eye on emerging trends, and think long-term. Your journey to financial freedom is not just about immediate gains but creating a lasting legacy that benefits not only you but future generations as well.

Your path to financial freedom is a marathon, not a sprint. But with the right mindset, tools, and strategies, you're well-equipped to reach the finish line. Keep pushing forward, stay resilient, and embrace the limitless potential that lies ahead. Your journey has just begun, and the possibilities are endless.

Appendix A:
Resources for Further Learning

Embarking on a journey to financial freedom is a continuous learning experience. The more you know, the more equipped you are to build and manage multiple streams of passive income. Below, you'll find a curated list of resources to deepen your understanding and propel you forward.

Books

Rich Dad Poor Dad by Robert T. Kiyosaki - A classic that introduces key financial concepts that are foundational for building passive income.

Your Money or Your Life by Vicki Robin and Joe Dominguez - A deep dive into transforming your relationship with money and achieving financial independence.

The Intelligent Investor by Benjamin Graham - Essential reading for understanding stock market investments.

Crushing It! by Gary Vaynerchuk - Insightful for those looking to leverage social media platforms and personal branding as part of their passive income strategy.

The Millionaire Real Estate Investor by Gary Keller - A must-read if you're considering real estate as a primary avenue for passive income.

Podcasts

The Tim Ferriss Show - Offers valuable insights on optimizing productivity and various income strategies.

Smart Passive Income by Pat Flynn - Covers a broad range of passive income techniques, with actionable advice and expert interviews.

BiggerPockets Real Estate Podcast - Focused specifically on real estate investing, perfect for both novices and seasoned investors.

Invest Like the Best by Patrick O'Shaughnessy - Engaging conversations around investment strategies with top performers in the field.

Online Courses

Udemy - Offers a plethora of courses on topics ranging from stock investing to affiliate marketing, tailored to various skill levels.

Coursera - Features courses from top universities on financial markets, digital marketing, and more.

Skillshare - Provides numerous classes on creative skills and business strategies, essential for building digital products.

LinkedIn Learning - A great resource for learning about entrepreneurship, finance, and marketing strategies.

Websites and Blogs

Investopedia - Comprehensive guides and tutorials on various financial instruments and investment strategies.

BiggerPockets - A wealth of information on real estate investing, complete with forums and calculators.

Neil Patel's Blog - Expert advice on digital marketing, SEO, and building online businesses.

Mr. Money Mustache - Offers practical advice and community support for achieving financial independence through frugality and smart investments.

Financial Samurai - Insightful articles on personal finance, investment strategies, and achieving financial freedom.

YouTube Channels

Graham Stephan - Covers a variety of financial topics, including real estate and stock market investing.

Pat Flynn - Offers tutorials and case studies on building passive income streams through online business.

Ali Abdaal - Productivity and financial independence tips, with a focus on building multiple income streams.

Meet Kevin - Provides insights into real estate investing, stock market updates, and personal finance advice.

Andrei Jikh - Focuses on personal finance and investing, making complex topics accessible to everyone.

Communities and Forums

Reddit - Subreddits like **r/financialindependence** and **r/passive_income** are treasure troves of shared experiences and advice.

BiggerPockets Forums - A vibrant community where real estate investors of all levels share insights and support each other.

Early Retirement Extreme Forum - Focused on extreme early retirement, frugality, and unconventional strategies for achieving financial independence.

Money Mustache Forums - Engaging discussions on achieving financial independence through low-cost living and smart investing.

By leveraging these resources, you'll be well on your way to mastering the skills needed to build and sustain your passive income streams. Remember, continuous learning and adaptability are crucial components of long-term success in this journey.

Appendix B:
Checklist for Starting Your Passive Income Journey

Embarking on a journey to create multiple streams of passive income can seem daunting, but having a clear roadmap can make all the difference. Use this checklist to ensure you're covering the essential steps to set yourself up for long-term financial success. Ready to dive in? Let's get started!

1. Understand Passive Income

Research different types of passive income streams (e.g., digital products, rental income, investment dividends).

Analyze real-world examples of successful passive income ventures to understand the myth vs. reality.

2. Shift Your Mindset

Embrace the transition from active earnings to building passive wealth.

Work on cultivating patience and persistence; remember, passive income often takes time to build.

Address and overcome any fears or doubts you have about embarking on this journey.

3. Lay the Foundation

Set clear, long-term financial goals for your passive income streams.

Understand your current financial starting point, including assets, liabilities, and net worth.

Invest time in enhancing your financial literacy to make informed decisions.

4. Explore Real Estate Opportunities

Research and identify the best locations for rental properties.

Look into financing options for your first property purchase.

Consider REITs and short-term rentals like Airbnb as alternative real estate investment strategies.

5. Create Digital Products

Identify your niche and target audience for digital products.

Start with eBooks or online courses, crafting compelling and valuable content.

Plan your marketing strategy to effectively promote and sell your digital products.

6. Invest in the Stock Market

Learn the basics of dividends and how they contribute to passive income.

Build a diversified dividend portfolio to generate steady income.

Explore ETFs and mutual funds as part of your investment strategy.

7. Master Affiliate Marketing

Select profitable niches that align with your interests and expertise.

Build an affiliate website with engaging content to drive traffic.

Implement SEO strategies to increase visibility and attract organic traffic.

8. Set Up a Dropshipping Business

Create an online store using platforms like Shopify or WooCommerce.

Find reliable suppliers to ensure product quality and timely delivery.

Automate order fulfillment to streamline your operations.

9. Start a Blog

Choose a niche and develop a content strategy to attract and retain readers.

Explore different monetization options, such as advertising revenue and sponsored content.

10. Leverage Social Media

Understand different revenue streams available on platforms like YouTube and Instagram.

Consider podcasting as a means to generate passive income.

11. Build an Email List

Create an enticing lead magnet to attract subscribers.

Design effective email campaigns to engage your audience.

Set up automated sequences to maintain consistent communication with your subscribers.

12. Explore Advanced Strategies

Look into licensing your intellectual property for recurring revenue.

Consider silent business partnerships to gain passive income without daily involvement.

Research high-yield savings and peer-to-peer lending platforms as additional income sources.

13. Optimize and Scale

Diversify your income streams to minimize risk and maximize earnings.

Consistently analyze your profits and reinvest wisely.

Consider outsourcing and automation to free up your time and scale your operations.

14. Stay Legal

Set up the right business structure for your passive income ventures.

Understand and comply with tax regulations and other legal requirements.

Take steps to protect your assets through appropriate legal measures.

15. Maintain Balance

Set clear boundaries between work and personal life.

Prioritize self-care to avoid burnout and maintain productivity.

Embrace continuous learning to stay ahead in your passive income journey.

This checklist is your starting point; refer back to it often as you move forward. Every step you take brings you closer to the financial freedom you seek.

Glossary of Terms

Welcome to the Glossary of Terms. This section is your go-to reference for understanding the key terminologies you'll encounter throughout your journey to financial freedom through passive income generation. Whether you're diving into the world of real estate, digital products, or investment dividends, mastering these terms will propel you forward with confidence and clarity.

Affiliate Marketing

A performance-based marketing strategy where individuals earn a commission by promoting other people's or companies' products. Affiliates earn income by driving traffic and sales through unique affiliate links.

Airbnb

An online marketplace that connects people who want to rent out their homes with those looking for accommodations. It allows property owners to earn rental income from short-term stays.

Automated Order Fulfillment

The process of using technology and third-party services to handle the logistics of processing and shipping orders, commonly used in e-commerce and dropshipping businesses. This frees up time for business owners to focus on other aspects of their business.

Blog Monetization

The methods by which a blog generates income. This can include advertising revenue, sponsored content, affiliate marketing, and selling products or services directly to readers.

Cash Flow

The net amount of cash being transferred into and out of a business. It is a crucial metric for assessing the liquidity, flexibility, and overall financial health of a business.

Dividend

A payment made by a corporation to its shareholders, usually in the form of cash or additional stock. Dividends are typically distributed from profits and are a common form of passive income for investors.

Digital Products

Products that are sold and distributed electronically, such as eBooks, online courses, software, and mobile applications. These products often require an initial investment of time and resources but can generate ongoing revenue with minimal additional effort.

Drop Shipping

A retail fulfillment method where a store doesn't keep the products it sells in stock. Instead, it purchases the item from a third party and has it shipped directly to the customer. As a result, the seller never handles the product directly.

Email Marketing

A direct marketing strategy that uses email to promote products or services. It is an effective tool for building relationships with potential and current customers, and it often involves list building and lead magnets.

ETF (Exchange-Traded Fund)

An investment fund traded on stock exchanges, much like stocks. ETFs typically hold assets such as stocks, commodities, or bonds and generally operate with an arbitrage mechanism designed to keep trading close to its net asset value.

Financial Freedom

The status of having sufficient personal wealth to live without needing to work actively for basic necessities. It is achieved by building and managing multiple streams of passive income.

Investment Dividends

Payments made to shareholders from a corporation's earnings. These distributions are a common passive income source for investors holding shares in dividend-paying companies.

Lead Magnet

A free item or service given away to gather contact details. Examples include eBooks, whitepapers, and webinars. It is commonly used in email marketing to build a subscriber list.

Passive Income

Income that requires minimal effort to maintain once the initial work is completed. Common sources include rental income, dividends, and digital product sales. It allows for financial freedom by providing ongoing revenue without continuous active work.

REIT (Real Estate Investment Trust)

A company that owns, operates, or finances income-producing real estate. REITs provide a way for individual investors to earn a share of the income produced through commercial real estate ownership without actually buying, managing, or financing any properties themselves.

SEO (Search Engine Optimization)

The process of optimizing a website to rank higher in search engine results pages (SERPs). It involves improving the site's content, structure, and technical performance to increase organic (non-paid) traffic.

Side Hustle

An additional job or work activity that a person engages in outside of their full-time employment to supplement their income. Many people start side hustles with the goal of eventually turning them into full-time passive income streams.

Sovereignty

In the financial context, it refers to the autonomy and resilience gained through diversified income streams, allowing an individual to make life choices without being overly dependent on a single source of income.

Sponsored Content

Content that is created for a brand or company in exchange for monetary compensation. It is a common method of blog monetization where bloggers promote a product or service to their audience.

Webinar

A seminar conducted over the internet. Webinars are often used to deliver educational content, generate leads, and engage with customers in real-time. They can also serve as an effective lead magnet.

Use this glossary as a resource to guide you through the complex landscape of passive income generation. Understanding these terms will be instrumental in navigating your path toward financial independence and long-term success.

www.ingramcontent.com/pod-product-compliance
Lightning Source LLC
Chambersburg PA
CBHW031840170526
45157CB00001B/367